Educator's Podcast Guide

Bard Williams

International Society for Technology in Education
EUGENE, OREGON • WASHINGTON, DC

Educator's Podcast Guide
Bard Williams

Acquisitions Editor: *Scott Harter* Copy Editor: *Mary Snyder*
Production Editor: *Lynda Gansel* Cover Design: *Signe Landin*
Production Coordinator: *Maddelyn High* Book Design and Production: *Kim McGovern*
Graphic Designer: *Signe Landin*
Rights and Permissions Administrator: *Diane Durrett*

Library of Congress Cataloging-in-Publication Data

Williams, Bard.
   Educator's podcast guide / Bard Williams. — 1st ed.
      p. cm.
   ISBN 978-1-56484-231-2 (pbk.)
   1. Internet in education. 2. Podcasting. 3. Educational innovations.   I. International
Society for Technology in Education. II. Title.
   LB1044.87.W53 2007
   371.33'44678—dc22

                                                                    2007013280

First Edition
ISBN: 978-1-56484-231-2

Printed in the United States of America

International Society for Technology in Education (ISTE)
Washington, DC, Office:
      1710 Rhode Island Ave. NW, Suite 900, Washington, DC 20036-3132
Eugene, Oregon, Office:
      175 West Broadway, Suite 300, Eugene, OR 97401-3003
Order Desk: 1.800.336.5191
Order Fax: 1.541.302.3778
Customer Service: orders@iste.org
Book Publishing: books@iste.org
Rights and Permissions: permissions@iste.org
Web: www.iste.org

About ISTE

The International Society for Technology in Education (ISTE) is the trusted source for professional development, knowledge generation, advocacy, and leadership for innovation. A nonprofit membership association, ISTE provides leadership and service to improve teaching, learning, and school leadership by advancing the effective use of technology in PK–12 and teacher education.

Home of the National Educational Technology Standards (NETS), the Center for Applied Research in Educational Technology (CARET), and the National Educational Computing Conference (NECC), ISTE represents more than 85,000 professionals worldwide. We support our members with information, networking opportunities, and guidance as they face the challenge of transforming education. To find out more about these and other ISTE initiatives, visit our Web site at **www.iste.org**.

As part of our mission, ISTE Book Publishing works with experienced educators to develop and produce practical resources for classroom teachers, teacher educators, and technology leaders. Every manuscript we select for publication is carefully peer-reviewed and professionally edited. We look for content that emphasizes the effective use of technology where it can make a difference—increasing the productivity of teachers and administrators; helping students with unique learning styles, abilities, or backgrounds; collecting and using data for decision making at the school and district levels; and creating dynamic, project-based learning environments that engage 21st-century learners. We value your feedback on this book and other ISTE products. E-mail us at **books@iste.org**.

About the Author

Bard Williams, Ed.D.

While a sophomore at the University of Georgia, Bard Williams dropped a box full of computer punch cards down the steps of the Graduate Studies building. It took nearly a week to painstakingly reorder the cards. He re-ran the job on the school's "high-tech" computers and received his obligatory 100-page green bar printout—only to find out that the program quit executing after the 5th card! This could have been the end of his interest in technology. Luckily, it wasn't.

Bard went on to enjoy a career as a middle school and college educator, a writer, and a technology "explorer." He is the author of more than 10 books, including ISTE's bestselling *Palm Handheld Computers: A Complete Resource for Classroom Teachers* (co-author), and *We're Getting Wired, We're Going Mobile, What's Next?*; the award-winning *Internet for Teachers*, published by IDG Books; and more than 300 articles.

In his spare time, he recharges his energy by speaking at educational conferences, teaching, and running a successful Silicon Valley education and creative marketing & consulting company called Techthree (www.techthree.com).

Acknowledgement

This book would not have been possible without learning ideas and resources available from Apple and those participating in the "iPod economy" across the Internet. In addition to the thousands of wonderful podcasters out there, I'd like to thank the education team at Palm for providing resources and information about using mobile devices for podcasting, and the Palm "PETCs" who eagerly contributed sites to the book.

I'd also like to thank members of the ISTE family—especially Scott Harter and Jennifer Ragan-Fore—and all those who worked hard to make this work as useful and up-to-date as possible.

Finally, I'd like to thank my family and friends for their encouragement and support—Gina Adams, P.B. Adams and my muse, Regis Costa, in particular. Works like this steal many hours from "home time" and I continue to be grateful for a loving group of people who understand.

Dedication

This book is dedicated to my nephews Joshua and Zachary Wilson who will undoubtedly change the world with their enthusiasm and ambition.

Other ISTE books by Bard Williams

> *Handheld Computers and Smartphones in Secondary Schools: A Guide to Hands-on Learning*

> *Palm Handheld Computers: A Complete Resource for Classroom Teachers*

Contents

How to Use This Book

This book is for anyone who's involved in using, supporting, or evangelizing technology in an education institution. It's designed as a quick and ready reference for educators and students who span the continuum from newbie to expert in the world of podcasting.

This book is part user-manual, part curriculum planning tool, and part implementation survival guide. I've included several chapters with foundational information because, as with any new technology, knowing a bit about the basics is essential for success. The bulk of the book, however, is a directory of information about podcasts you'll want to check out for use in your curriculum, with other educators, or for personal knowledge growth.

The book is organized as a quick reference, so you can glance at the table of contents and zip in and out of chapters as needed. I'd recommend, however, that you read chapters 1 and 2 first for a foundation for your discussions with others about implementation and to ensure you realize, and can articulate, the benefits of podcast technology.

Part I gives you the quick "need-to-know" about podcasting and an overview of how you might expand and enhance curriculum content with podcasts. There's also a discussion about evaluating podcasts for use in education.

In **Part II**, you get to the heart of the matter with a smorgasbord of education-related podcasts, sorted for your use by curriculum area. You'll also find podcasts for higher education and educational technology.

Tips are little pieces of information and random ideas that I just couldn't keep to myself. Often, these tips can save you a lot of time.

Sidebars contain information that is relevant but not necessarily essential to understanding the chapter. These sidebars are often a paragraph or more in length and build upon information in the text. These are great reading if you just have a second or two between classes or IT meetings.

The **Appendixes** contain a "directory of directories" so you can easily find more sites after you've checked out the ones in this book. There is also a list of all the National Educational Technology Standards for Students and Teachers.

However you jump in, I hope this book is as much fun for you to read as it was for me to write (and it was very fun to write)! Use it as a catalyst for your thinking and a jumping off point for your first, or next, podcast. Enjoy!

Podcasting »
What Are You
Waiting For?

FINALLY—A TECHNOLOGY that helps bridge the gap between content delivery and the video game generation. The podcast blends the beauty of topical research and knowledge collection with a radio- or TV-style presentation perfect for the short attention span of many of our students (and fellow educators).

This part of the book presents a general introduction to podcasting; an overview of how to listen to and create your own podcasts; some practical ideas for incorporating podcast content into your curriculum; and a word or three about selecting and evaluating podcast content.

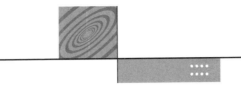

CHAPTER 1

Introduction to Podcasting

It's nice now and then when something new comes along that really takes technology and education to a new level. Podcasting, the ability to create or listen to audio or video content via the Web on your desktop or mobile computer, just might be that "something new" that energizes your classroom and breathes even more excitement into your favorite lesson plans. This chapter takes you step-by-step through an introduction to the new technology. You'll march through information about finding podcasts, listening to podcasts and, for the eager, creating and posting your own podcasts.

Content in Your Pocket

Scientists are studying locusts and their uncanny ability to avoid car windshields and using that science to build collision-avoidance systems for humans. This according to a podcast from BBC's Naked Scientists (www.thenakedscientists.com).

In Chris Hoovler's Sixth Grade podcast, originating from Freedom Middle School in Fredericksburg, VA, there's a secret word hidden on the school's Web site. If you listen to the band podcast featuring the school's students playing at their best, you'll get the word. Give the secret word to the teacher before homeroom and earn a prize. The students sound great and I spent 10 minutes looking for the secret word—and finding out more about their very cool school (www.myfreedomband.org).

Zebras don't get ulcers. Stanford University's Dr. Robert Sapolsky points out that zebras don't get ulcers, but they get lots of other things like nasty intestinal disorders. People get more odd maladies and unlike what our ancestors experienced, our diseases slowly build up over time. In a very compelling lecture originally delivered to a group of senior citizens, Dr. Sapolsky tells us that lots of our problems today are caused or exacerbated by stress (http://itunes.stanford.edu).

Don't rely on the films that have been shown continuously in classrooms since 1962. Host Dan Schmit, from the College of Education at the University of Nebraska in Lincoln, encourages teachers to download and sample podcasts to spice things up. Dan runs marathons and has created "sound-seeing tour" podcasts, recorded using his cell phone during races. On the podcast Web site (www.intelligenic.com/blog/), he supports the community with fundraising for the Leukemia and Lymphoma Society.

What is Podcasting?

Podcasting is the ability to create or listen to audio or video content, called a *podcast*, via the Web, either live, or downloaded for later viewing/ listening on your desktop, laptop computer, or on a mobile device like a smartphone or many MP3 players like the Apple iPod. Podcasting has been around in one form or another since 2004, when podcasts were audio-only and tough to find on the Internet. In June of 2005, podcasting jumped from relative obscurity into "the next big thing" when Apple released iTunes (v4.9) which offered fully integrated podcast support. The word "podcast" was even selected by the editors of the New Oxford American Dictionary as the Word of the Year for 2005. Overnight, finding the content and getting it on your listening device became as easy as finding the next tune from U2.

Downloading a podcast is different from downloading regular audio and video files from a Web site because, in general, the content is routinely or regularly updated, and you can receive new content via subscription. Wikipedia provides a thorough discussion of podcasting (http://en.wikipedia.org/wiki/Podcast/).

Besides the introduction of Apple's easy-to-use tools, there was also a sudden explosion in broadband connectivity, storage space and computer memory. Downloading media-rich content became the rule instead of the exception and people began to post movies and audio files all over the Web. It was just a matter of time before podcasting really caught on.

The Podcast Attraction

Students love podcasts because podcasts are:

> available anytime, even on the way to the mall

> more compelling than some of the other classroom activities

> great for people who learn better by listening

> easy to access

> changing all the time

> easy to create and post

Jump ahead to 2007 and welcome the world of *time-shifted content*. Thousands of podcasts are available via the Internet, easy to find and ready to listen to whenever you need them. For students and teachers, this means you can build libraries of content and have them ready for storage, or produce your own podcasts for parents, other students, or your community.

As with most technologies, especially the fun ones, you and your students have the option of moving across the spectrum of use of the technology from content consumers (those who listen to podcast content) to content producers (those who produce and distribute their own podcasts). As you learn more about podcasting, you will probably reach a point where you want to create your own. Not only because it's fun, but because it opens so many more doors to creatively enhancing your curriculum. It also speaks to other learning styles.

Podcasting offers options for learners with diverse learning needs and many learning styles. If the podcast is a video podcast, it offers the visual learner an option for review and reflection. The auditory learner can play and replay content indefinitely. The kinesthetic learner can play the time-shifted content outside of school when movement is free. Podcasts can be a boon to those working with students who have special learning needs too. Podcasts offer another alternative to engage the digital student.

The advances in technology and consumer bandwidth have also created opportunities for more media-rich content like video. Video podcasts, also called *vodcasts*, are becoming more prevalent. While this book focuses primarily on podcasts, most of the information presented about classroom use is applicable to vodcasts.

One common misconception is that you must have a mobile MP3 player (like an iPod) to listen to a podcast. Not true. All you need is a computer and access to the Internet. Many people listen to podcasts on their desktop or laptop computer.

Getting Started

The best way to start your podcast experience is to kick back and listen to a few. This book offers quite a few teacher-tested sites to get you started. If you want to try a sample before you move on to learn more about podcasting, just skip ahead a few chapters and find a podcast you like. Each podcast in the directory features a Web site you can visit, then click a link to listen to the podcast using your browser or download to your favorite mobile device. It's easy. Really.

Listening to an audio podcast is a lot like listening to your car radio. You just need to know how to tune in all the content out there.

The steps to getting a podcast from the provider to your eyes and ears are really quite simple. Here's a summary:

Search for podcasts using your Web browser, or podcast aggregators like Apple's iTunes or obtain a podcast address from other places like magazines, billboards, or this book.

Visit the Web site and search for a "click to listen," "play," or "download" button. You'll have the option to listen to or view the podcast directly on your desktop or save it in a format that allows for transfer to a mobile listening device like an iPod or audio/video-capable smartphone.

Subscribe to the podcast if you like it and it's a podcast presented in a series. You can arrange for this automatic transfer of upcoming podcasts through your browser, iTunes or other podcast tool.

FINDING PODCASTS

There are quite a few ways to find podcasts on the Internet. One way is to use software such as Apple's iTunes and scan the built-in dynamic directory of thousands of podcasts. With iTunes, you can also search by name, category, or check out the podcasts that get the most downloads (most popular among iTunes users). If you don't see what you need in Apple's list, then you can use a search engine to search a topic (e.g., podcast middle school discipline) and copy and paste the podcast URL (Web address) into iTunes. Podcasts, it turns out, have addresses similar to Web sites on the Internet. They're a bit different in that they often end in "xml" or "MP3" instead of "html," but they work the same way.

There are other handy software tools to help make finding and listening to podcasts even easier. For example, in iTunes just choose the Podcasts item from the left navigation menu, then click the arrow next to Podcast Directory at the bottom of the window (figure 1.1). If you don't have iTunes program installed on your computer, you can download it for free (available for Mac OS and Microsoft Windows) from Apple at www.apple.com/itunes/). If you've got a dial-up connection, it will take a little while to download the iTunes 7 program, but once it's done, it works fairly quickly.

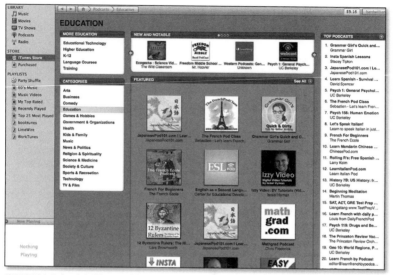

FIGURE 1.1 Apple's iTunes offers a well-organized podcast directory and an easy way to listen to podcasts on your computer, or transfer them to your iPod.

The majority of the podcast audience uses iTunes. The program has many benefits for podcast listeners and viewers including:

> the ability to easily search and locate podcasts by category or content

> support for Mac OS and Windows

> a legendary user-interface that makes choosing and down-loading podcast content as easy as a click of the mouse—no long URLs needed

> a library-based architecture that makes the complex task of sorting your podcasts simple

> an easy way to subscribe to and organize podcasts using the same *playlist* you use to organize your music or videos

Of course, the easiest way to jump into podcast exploration is to search later chapters in this book. There you'll find a list of popular and teacher- and student-tested links for your exploration pleasure. It will give you a good start at sifting through the thousands of podcasts and offer you the "good stuff" and save you lots of time. Just choose a podcast, launch your favorite Web browser, visit the URL, and search for the podcast by title.

More tools, such as Juice, Podcast Tuner, and NewsFire, continue to become available—most for free. While iTunes is arguably the easiest to use, it's nice to know you have other (also free) options. You'll find a longer list of podcatchers later in this chapter.

A SUBSCRIPTION, PLEASE!

Now that you've located a podcast and decided you'd like to see or hear more, you have to log in every day, week or whenever and download the next edition of the program, right? Nope! iTunes and many other podcast programs allow you to *subscribe* to podcast streams you like. That means at an interval controlled by you, your device automatically receives and archives new content as it's available and it's sitting there waiting for you when you're ready. If you use an iPod, you can even set the downloaded content to automatically transfer to the device every time you connect your iPod to your computer.

The technology used to subscribe is called RSS (Really Simple Syndication) and is the same technology used to deliver those crawling dynamic news feeds you see on sites like CNN or Apple. RSS is also used to update you automatically when someone posts to a blog you're subscribed to. In fact, the whole podcast subscription process works much like a blog, except that it's audio or video content you're getting instead of text and graphics.

Making Your Own Podcasts

If you're anything like me, once you get your hands on a new technology you want to start using it and making it your own. Of course you want to make your own podcasts—you're a lifelong learner! I have good news. It's not too tough to do.

Like many other Internet-related technologies, podcasting has entered the mainstream with a suite of ever-growing, ever-improving tools. This means that creating a basic audio or video podcast is very easy.

IT'S EASY TO MAKE A PODCAST, BUT SHOULD YOU?

This is probably a good place for a quick flashback to the beginning of the Web. First there were the mavericks and early adopters who posted cool content. Then mainstream tools came along, bringing easy Web site creation, and strange and sometimes inane content began to proliferate. People posted Web sites just because they could (remember the same syndrome in the early days of desktop publishing?) and the focus turned to adding bells and whistles in a mad rush to improve traffic to Web sites.

Some people forgot that one of the most compelling reasons that Web publishing exists is to provide content that's actually interesting, informative, entertaining and/or useful.

Podcasts are entering that era too. Just because you or your students *can* create a podcast doesn't mean you *should*. From an educational perspective, it makes good sense to help students learn to use the tools needed to create and listen to or view podcasts. It also makes sense to put the focus right from the beginning on where it belongs—on the content.

PODCAST CREATION PRIMER

The best podcasts show forethought and are presented in a logical manner—with a little bit of production value. It's that production value, which sometimes takes less work that you'd think, that will keep people coming back to your podcast. Here's a very brief primer on creating your best podcast.

Creating a podcast is basically a six-step process:

1. plan the content and "flow" of your podcast
2. research and collect the information and write the scripts or prepare video assets
3. record your podcast
4. post your podcast
5. tell the world
6. evaluate your podcast and plan for improvement (if needed)

Planning

If you and your students have ever produced a student newscast for airing over the public-address system in your school, or created a video yearbook or other content-focused video, DVD, or CD, you know all you need to produce content for a podcast.

A good place to begin is writing a brief one- or two-sentence statement that encompasses the format, purpose and audience for your podcast. Here's an example one teacher used:

> The purpose of our audio podcast is to offer daily updates of news and information from our school to our parents and community.

Nice and succinct, huh?

Here's an example from a science teacher:

> Our video podcast provides basic information about ecology and our community to students.

The next step is a content outline. Don't worry, this is much more fun than planning a five-paragraph theme. Your content outline should offer general statements, bullets, or snippets of info about what you want to present and the order that you want to present it. If you're really on the ball, this outline becomes what professional broadcasters call a *run-down*.

Here's an example of a run-down for a 10-minute podcast for technology coordinators. In case you're unfamiliar with some of the broadcast-speak, I've defined some terms in the Recording and Polishing the Podcast section of this chapter. Of course, you may want your outline to be much more detailed. The times are critical, though, to keep your show on track.

> **» TIP**
>
> **TOO MUCH OF GOOD THING**
>
> The average attention span of most students (and their parents) is getting shorter. Think about beginning with SHORT podcasts of 15 minutes or less. Save the longer podcasts for those who teach or provide lots of critical, compelling, or need-to-know information.

SUPPORTING HANDHELD TECHNOLOGY IN SCHOOLS

(Times below represent how far into the podcast the event happens)

0:00:   Podcast open (intro music, program intro by P.C. Jones)

0:45:   Podcast content (Jane Presenter)

2:30:   Issues and challenges of handheld technology

4:00:   Break—teaser/tip or info on next podcast

4:20:   Building an effective support system

8:00:   10 steps to world-class support of handheld devices

9:40:   Podcast recap (P.C. Jones)

9:55:   Podcast close (exit music)

If you or your students plan to publish a regular podcast, it makes sense to offer a common identity or "brand" for your podcast. That means openings and closings are done the same way, music is the same, and you ALWAYS let the listener/viewer know the name and location of your school within the first minute—and at the last minute—of your podcast.

›› TIP

INTERESTING INTERVIEWS

There's only one way to get good at interviewing. Practice. Set up sample interviews where students record their voices interviewing other students on current topics of interest. End the activity with a list of "do's and don'ts" for good interviewing technique.

Research, Asset Collection, and Scripting

Any good podcast begins with a bit of research. It may be collection of news content; collection of assets, such as audio or video segments; or information like interviews, bibliographic citations, etc.

If you're including interviews in your podcast, you will probably need to edit the recordings. You can use Apple's Garage Band or the freeware Audacity, for example, to cut and paste audio content, or iMovie to edit your video content or add credits.

You'll also need to select royalty-free or licensed music snippets for your introduction and closing segments.

As with any media production, you'll need to identify your production team. You'll need the "talent" (broadcast-speak for the host), speakers/actors to present content, a producer to take what you record and edit it into your final piece, and a Webmaster to upload your content to a site and make it accessible to others. Like every other "you should have a bunch of people to do this" activity you read about in technology books, the exception is often education. The reality is that it's very likely that one person (that would be you) wears each and every hat. At least you'll have total control over the final product!

The purpose of collecting and researching information is to create a script. Even if your podcast is an open interview format, you'll still need a basic set of information that fits your run-down (see the Planning section).

> **» | TIP**
>
> **DEVELOP YOUR TALENT**
>
> Because your podcast is your calling card to the world, consider "auditioning" students to be the host and speaker of your regular podcasts. Listen for clear articulation, a good delivery rate, and an enthusiastic, but not out of control, delivery. Just like in the school play, the lead roles really do make a difference.

Be sure you and your students always think about a person who represents your audience. If your podcast is for class presentation, then make sure students write and speak as they would to their peers. If it's for parents, suggest they write, produce, and speak thinking of their own parents.

Recording and Polishing the Podcast

The production of your podcast is very similar to the production of the daily audio or video news and announcements you might enjoy over your school's public-address system.

To build your own podcast, you need just a few tools—most you probably already have:

> computer
> computer software that can capture digital audio or video and allow at least basic editing
> a microphone (built-in or external)
> headphones (optional, but recommended)
> a digital video camera (if your podcast is a vodcast)
> a place on a file server to host your podcast
> a script or show run-down

For an in-depth discussion of these tools, see the Hardware and Software Needs section of this chapter.

Here are a few essential elements that can help keep listeners on track and interested:

›› TIP

GET TO THE POINT

Any good journalist will tell you that it's the first 30 seconds of content that keeps people tuned in to a TV or radio show, and the first few sentences in print. Podcasts are no different. Avoid the urge to do two-minute guitar solos for your theme song (I'd suggest less than 15 seconds for music) and get to the point quickly.

Intro/exit music. Use short snippets of music to identify the opening and close of your podcast. The music serves three purposes: to brand your podcast, to cue users to the beginning and end of the podcast, and to set the tone for the type of content you present. Music should be short in length (10–15 seconds) and royalty free or used with permission. Your band or music teacher may be able to offer options for recording your own. Student contests are a fun way to get a theme song too. Music can make a huge difference in setting the tone of your podcast so be sure to match the music to the podcast's style and spirit. Use an up-tempo instrumental, for example, to intro a student newscast, or a more serene pastoral excerpt to intro a series on serious local issues.

Program intro. This is where a third party (*host*) introduces the podcast and sets the stage with essential information. Elements of a good introduction include:

> name of the podcast

> date and/or episode or volume number of the podcast (if appropriate)

> location and or originator (author) of the podcast

> name of the host

> purpose (very brief) of the podcast

Here's an example:

> Welcome to Tech Coordinator 101, ISTE's podcast series that helps school and district coordinators keep up to date with issues and challenges of implementing technology in schools. I'm your host, Bard Williams, and this is the second podcast in the series. Today's podcast originates from ISTE headquarters in Oregon and is entitled "Supporting handheld technology in schools."

In a video podcast, the information above could be presented as text over a video montage or with a voice-over—it's like the opening credits of a newscast you might see on TV.

Podcast teaser. Before a short break in the content to advertise an upcoming event, "tease" your audience with what's coming next, or present a useful tip. Here's an example:

> Coming up next, you'll hear Chip Motherboard talk about the newest computers for education and later, Red Riding Hood will fill us in on what's new in iMovie making. But first, our tip of the day: Did you know that you can easily add sound effects to your next podcast? Here's how... <insert content>.

> You're listening to the <podcast name> podcast from <city, state> and this is your host <hostname>. Let's return to our guest <guest name>.

Podcast recap. Thank your listeners for tuning in, remind users of the information in the intro, and "tease" future podcasts (optional). Here's an example:

> You've been listening (watching) Tech Coordinator 101, ISTE's podcast series that helps school and district coordinators keep up to date with the issues and challenges of implementing technology in schools. This program, entitled "Supporting handheld technology in schools," is the second in a series. To learn more, visit www.iste.org and click the podcasts link.

Even if your podcast is short—say, less than 15 minutes—it's a good idea to offer the listener more than one speaker. Try either a host and speaker pair, or multiple speakers. That variety can keep your listeners riveted to your content and makes for a more interesting podcast. Most podcasters are eager to deliver information and that eagerness, especially in students, translates to a rapid rate of speech. Rehearsal, a bit of coaching, and a good script, always help.

›› TIP

BE QUIET

Ambient noise can kill a podcast. It makes for a distraction that can affect your ability to hear content clearly. Consider identifying a "sound proof booth" in your school where the recordings can be made. Book storage rooms, quiet conference rooms, or equipment storage rooms can be very quiet. You can also make a three-sided "recording station" in your classroom—kind of like a science fair diorama—but cover it with paper egg cartons to dampen noise and place a piece of cardboard over the top to kill noise from air conditioners. It's not optimal, but it works.

Hardware and Software Needs

Just about any modern computer will work for editing and producing your podcast. Because you might want to edit your content, particularly if it's video, you'll want lots of RAM (memory), adequate hard drive space and the fastest CPU you can get your hands on. That said, your two-year-old Powerbook or the Dell laptop in the closet is likely to have all you need in the way of power for producing podcasts.

Since podcasts end up as MP3 or MPEG/QT files (vodcasts), they're easy to archive. Think ahead about purchasing an external hard drive, or identifying a secure place on your school's network for storage. Organize them by the date they were published and/or by theme.

If you are creating a video podcast, you'll need to pay more attention to your computer setup. Lots of RAM and a fast processor make a huge difference with video editing and, of course, you'll need far more storage space for your video files than for audio-only.

PODCAST PRODUCTION SOFTWARE

The software component of podcasting allows you to capture sound (or images), edit them, and then save them into a format for podcasting.

Most podcasters use a software program called Audacity (http://audacity.sourceforge.net) to capture audio in an MP3 format. The program is open source, works with both PC and Mac, is free, and allows for basic audio editing. If you use Audacity, be sure to also download the MP3 encoder, there's a link on the Audacity site under Plug-ins.

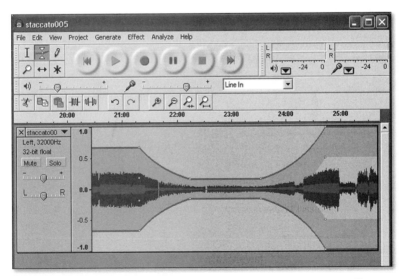

FIGURE 1.2 Audacity runs on both Windows and Mac and offers an easy recording interface. It's freeware, too!

Audacity offers the ability to do most basic editing tasks once your recording has been created. You can add a limited number of multiple tracks and cut, copy and paste segments of your audio.

If you're a Mac user, Apple's GarageBand works nicely too. Like Audacity, you can do all the basic editing you need, but unlike Audacity, you can create your own music. GarageBand, however, works much more like a professional audio tool and offers the tools to do much more, like add music you create, add more tracks, and play with lots of technical elements (tone, pitch and so on). If you're going to add music, GarageBand is great—just be sure that your music is *podsafe* (music that can be legally used in a podcast and freely distributed online for others to download).

FIGURE 1.3 Apple's GarageBand makes producing a professional sounding podcast very simple. Add your own theme music, fade sound in and out, and much more.

Windows users might want to check out Sony's free ACID Xpress (ACIDplanet.com).

For playback, you'll want to update your Windows Media Player or iTunes software. These are also referred to as *aggregators*, or more commonly as *podcatchers*. Both of the aforementioned podcatchers are free and it's a good idea to use these for playback because that's what most of your listeners will use.

Grabbing Your Podcasts with Podcatchers

Here's a short (but ever-changing) list of common podcast aggregators. Most of them are freeware and can be tracked down via your favorite search engine.

Linux/Open Source

Flashpopdder, Podget, PerlPodder, Bash iPodder, CastGrab, get_enclosures, pyPodder, jPodder, Jaeger, Podcatcher

Macintosh Podcast Software

iPodderX, iTunes, Jaeger, Juice, NewsFire, NetNewsWire, NewsMacPro, Playpod, Podcast Studio, Poddumfeeder, PodSafe, Pod2Go, PulpFiction, Yamipod

Online Services

MirPod, PodFeeder, Podcast Sender

Palm OS

QuickNews, iPodderSP, Smart Feed

Pocket PC

FeederReader

Windows Podcast Software

@Podder, AudioShell, BlogMatrix Sparks, CITA RSS Aggregator, CustomReader, Doppler, Golden Ear, HappyFish, iPodderX, iTunes, Jaeger, Juice, Newzee, NewzCrawler, nimiq, Podcast Amp, PodNova, Podsage, Podspider, Primetime Podcast, Pwopcatcher, Replay Radio, RSSRadio, Synclosure, TVTonic, WinAmp, Yamipod, Ziepod

If iTunes and Windows Media Player aren't to your liking, try indiepodder.org or podcastalley.com.

iPodder is a client application that allows you to subscribe to podcasts without using iTunes. Just download the application (it's free at www.ipodder.com) and double-click to go though the installation process.

Once iPodder is launched, just paste the RSS feed location into the "Add feed manually" form and click the scheduler tab to set the interval.

PODCAST PRODUCTION HARDWARE

Microphone

Believe it or not, the microphone is probably the single most important component of your podcast setup. Like radio, sound quality is critical if you want to get your message across. Some computers have built in microphones, and most offer an audio-in port that allows you to plug in a microphone for recording. A really inexpensive microphone will work, but it will also make you sound like you're speaking through a $2 walkie-talkie. If you plan on podcasting on a regular basis, you should definitely consider purchasing a good quality microphone. I recommend microphones from Shure.

Pop filter

You might also consider adding a pop filter to your setup. It's basically a nylon mesh stretched over a small frame that is positioned between you and your microphone. This helps eliminate the "pop" noise you hear when you speak words that contain plosive sounds (like "p," "t" and "k"). The crafty educator can create one from a simple wire coat hanger or embroidery hoop and some nylons.

You can also use most smartphones to capture audio, or add an attachment to your iPod and record directly to the player. Sound quality is not great, however. If you use a mobile device for recording, you can use Windows Media Player or iTunes to get the audio files to your desktop.

Headphones

Headphones allow you to hear the audio from your podcast in its purest form—without the interruptions of ambient noise. Headphones are important, particularly if you want to sound more professional, because they allow you to pick up and then use software to edit extraneous noise (like the fire engine that goes by on the street in front of your school) out of your podcast before you go live.

Server

The server is the final destination for the video or audio podcast you create. It represents a place on the Internet where the actual files will be stored and offers an address so that others can find and download your podcast. The server is also the place where you place files to make your podcast subscribable using RSS (Really Simple Syndication).

If you don't have your own Web site, you'll need to find a Web hosting site and register a domain name (e.g., www.whatever.com). Most school districts have .edu domains that offer plenty of server space for your podcast content. It's best to reserve at least 4 gigabytes (4 GB) of storage to be sure you have plenty room for all your files. Check with your district's IT director, or your local school technology coordinator for information about what's available.

You can also use one of the free posting sites, like Blogger (owned by Google) or Liberation Syndication (LibSyn) to create a *blog* (Weblog). The blog format is perfect for posting audio and video podcasts because the typical blog allows for uploading data in chunks (like you would entries in a diary) and then

How Much Space?

To figure out how much space you might ultimately need, try this simple formula: podcast length x bytes per minute.

Podcast bytes per minute depends on your encoding rate: 96 kbps (good for most podcasts). At this bit rate, the file size is about 0.7 MB per minute.

That means a 15-minute podcast, encoded at 0.7 MB per minute would fill about 10.5 MB on your host's hard drive. Multiply that by the number of podcasts you'll do and you'll get the estimated total space needed.

In general, a "talk only" podcast encoded at 64 kbps will occupy about 0.5 MB per minute on your hard drive. A "talk and music" at 96 kbps will take up about 0.7 MB/minute and a "mostly music" at 128 kbps will snap up 1 MB/minute.

Video podcasts are a very different animal as they can consume vast amounts of storage space. It's not unusual for a video podcast of 15 minutes to consume many gigabytes of space.

often that data is searchable. The downside of using a free posting site is that your URL will be longer and it's out of the control of your school or district personnel who are responsible for the quality and content of instruction-related materials. Both Blogger and Libsyn offer a service where you can register your own URL for about $10 a year.

Posting Podcasts and Finding Listeners

Distributing your podcast means finding a place to post (store on a computer accessible by others) your podcast file, and then making sure people can subscribe to your content.

> **›› TIP**
>
> **SCHEDULE IT**
>
> People might like your podcast the first time so much they'll want more. Consider setting a schedule and posting it on your school/ organization's website.

Finding a place to post your podcast is not that difficult. You can post them on your school or district servers, embed them in your blog (Blogger, for example, supports links to podcast content), or seek out a commercial ISP that will host the files.

If you've never published a blog before and you don't have a hosting provider, the easiest podcast setup might be Liberated Syndication (LibSyn), which is quite widely used in education. For about $5 per month LibSyn gives you the space and the tools necessary to distribute your podcast. If you plan on podcasting regularly, this is a good way to begin, but you should explore using your district's server—to save money and give you more control over the process in the long run.

There are other systems, like OurMedia, Podlot, Podbus and Audioblog, that are reliable and have the bandwidth to host your podcasts.

Once you've found a home for your podcast, you should submit it to search directories like iTunes so people can find your work. iTunes allows users to easily subscribe to your podcast.

To submit your podcast to iTunes, just click the "submit podcast" link on the main page of the Podcast page in the iTunes Music Store (accessible through iTunes on a Mac or PC). Enter the link for the RSS feed and fill in some specific info about your broadcast. Submitted podcasts don't immediately appear in the Music Store and may be reviewed before they are released in the directory. This review can take up to a week.

TELL THE WORLD

The cinematic adage "If you build it, they will come" is certainly NOT the case when it comes to any content on the Internet, including podcasts. Lots of beginning podcasters forget that if your audience extends beyond your local school or community, you'll have to be proactive in getting the word out. Getting the word out isn't difficult, but if you do it the wrong way, you'll get lost in the digital forest.

> **» TIP**
>
> **MAKE NOISE**
>
> Getting the word out about your published podcast is easier than you think. Tell your friends, share with professional organizations, publish an article about the process, or place your listing on web directories like iPodder.org.

Here are five ways to get your podcasts noticed:

1. **Viral marketing.** In the world of marketing, viral marketing refers to using your existing social networks to spread information quickly and inexpensively. In the case of schools, it means, essentially, arming your social network (teachers, students, parents) with information (press release or short blurb about your podcast) and having them spread it to all their friends. This is not, by the way, the same as spam because you'll only send to your friends and it's probably content they won't object to.

2. **Register/submit podcast to iTunes and other podcast directories.** Since iTunes is where many educators and the iPod community get their podcasting info, submitting your school or personal podcast to the iTunes podcast directory makes good sense.

3. **Use existing communications engines.** Your school probably has a school newsletter, so make sure you advertise your podcasts there. Make sure you also feature your podcast network at PTA meetings, school book fairs, and any other time you're communicating with your podcast's audience.

4. **Tag your blog.** If you have a blog, tag it with keywords that reflect the content of your podcast. Use terms as specific as possible. Since terms such as "education, student, class, curriculum" are often used, you should add specifics such as "early learning, physical science, writing process, calculus tutoring" to attract more traffic.

5. **Use other methods of communication.** Consider writing an article for your local newspaper or professional organization (like ISTE); or delivering a workshop at a conference (like NECC) to increase awareness and demand of your podcast.

» TIP

CONTROVERSY AND YOUR AUDIENCE

Sooner or later, a student or faculty member will want to speak their mind on some subject that you or your community might find controversial, in poor taste, or downright offensive. Head this off by adding podcast rules to your school's Acceptable Use Policy for Technology. You will thank me for this tip!

Evaluation

As with any activity or project, it's very useful to sit back and take a hard look at what you've produced. After you've aired your first podcast, you and your students should take a critical look at the content, technical elements, and "listenability" of your work. Your evaluation might involve informal polls of your audience, or more formal "grading."

Chapter 3 looks at ideas for evaluating podcasts created by your students, or those created by others. Using rubrics, you can help students hone in on what's important and improve delivery, timing, and much more.

The Next Step

Don't be too concerned if all the information in this chapter is overwhelming. The information in this book is designed to appeal to all levels of podcasters or would-be podcasters, and you can always go back and review things when you're ready.

If you're new to podcasting, your next step should be to log on to the Net and use iTunes or another directory to search out and listen to as many podcasts as you can. This will give you an idea of the breadth of content available, the production value of the podcasts (how they sound and how the content flows) and perhaps act as a wellspring of new ideas for you and your students.

In the next chapter, you can find out about how to actually incorporate podcasts into your curriculum, or use podcasts to enrich or enhance day-to-day activities in your school, district or community.

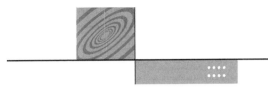

CHAPTER 2

Podcasts in the Classroom

It's easy to minimize podcasts as just another media resource in classrooms. While it's perfectly respectable to maintain a library of podcast content for access when the need arises, these audio or video resources are much more than just an encyclopedic source.

Much of the information presented in podcasts is highly topical and often time-sensitive. That means the resource has its biggest impact on teaching and learning in context and sometimes that context means the podcast works today during your lesson, but won't be relevant in two weeks.

A common example of a time-sensitive podcast is a daily or weekly school news and events report presented by your student council. The information is relevant for a short period and (sometimes) has little value after the relevance period has passed. This type of podcast does not need to be archived.

In other cases, say, a podcast featuring a series of live interviews from a sociologist exploring the Amazon jungle's native inhabitants, archiving and presenting the content when you're writing about or studying related topics makes sense.

Integrating Podcasts into Your Curriculum

All this is a relatively long-winded way of saying that, as with any classroom resource, podcasts are best used in the context of learning and not as an island of content.

The richness and immediacy of podcast content can add a whole new dimension to your curriculum. Today's dynamic podcast content can offer information not found in aging textbooks and offers an alternative to the more scholarly voice of most classroom resources. If you choose to *originate* podcasts, you can dramatically extend the reach and impact of meaningful classroom activities.

In general, there are as many ways for schools to use podcasts (either as consumer or producer) as there are to use most other classroom resources. All it takes is familiarity with the technology and a little vision. A scan of available podcasts and discussions with teachers using podcasts in the classroom revealed this starter list of suggestions for use:

> › curriculum enhancement

> › promote programs and activities

> › research

> › share school news

> › professional development

> › archived lessons (classroom recordings)

> field recording (field notes, interviews)
> study support (repetitive listening)

In the next few pages, you'll read more about each of these ideas for using podcasts in your classroom and maybe get some of your own!

CURRICULUM ENHANCEMENT

Podcasts can provide a wealth of information to expand and enhance your curriculum. Whether it's using a podcast to supply more information about a topic (reference), as a lesson starter (background), or as an extension of your lesson (enrichment), you'll find plenty of options in today's podcast-rich environment.

As with many other technologies, many educators feel most comfortable beginning with the incorporation of podcasts on a trial basis. Find an upcoming lesson, search for a podcast, and assign students to listen or view the podcast, then follow up with an activity, test of knowledge, or evaluation.

Here's an example. Christopher's eighth-grade science class is studying astronomy and they've just launched an activity to develop a timeline of space flight. Chris offers a NASA podcast (www.nasa.gov/podcast/) featuring updates on a current shuttle mission directly from the flight control center. A small group of students listens to the podcast, reports back to the class, and helps move the project forward. While this is a relatively low-level activity (à la Bloom), it helps students see (or hear) the value of podcast information and may prompt them to seek podcasts as a research tool for other projects.

In a more advanced lesson, a group of students in Karen's 11th-grade English literature class downloads four podcasts in which *King Lear* is read or reviewed and presents an evaluation, complete with samples played for the rest of the class, of how the play is interpreted, how production affects the understanding and enjoyment of the work, and how effective podcasting is in getting the theme of the work across. Karen's class likes the presentation so much they create their own podcast in which characters from *King Lear* are interviewed. The podcast is posted to the school's Web site and shared with other schools around the globe.

Audio or video podcasts are also perfect for painting a picture with words or images. The media allows you and your students to create vivid collections of thoughts and conversations, interviews and dramatic portrayals, and much more. While the idea of digital storytelling isn't at all new, the concept that these stories can be shared more easily, and in more formats, is a welcome enhancement.

See? While these are pretty simplistic explanations, you probably get the idea. On the lowest level, podcasts are research tools. Later, your students will begin to listen more critically, and then eventually start creating their own podcasts.

PROMOTING PROGRAMS AND ACTIVITIES

James couldn't wait for morning. As soon as he woke up, he rushed to his computer, disconnected his iPod (which had magically retrieved new data overnight) and listened to yesterday's play-by-play of the big football game between Shiloh and Parkview. The podcast allowed him to replay, over and over, the defining moment of the game when the opposing team's star receiver, Randy, caught a touchdown pass in the last seconds of the game only to find out he had stepped out of bounds. By the time breakfast was over, his two sisters, mom, and his friend Toby (who always eats breakfast with the family) had heard the excitement in the broadcaster's voice. James couldn't wait to get to school to talk about it.

> **» | TIP**
>
> **BEST OF THE WEB PODCASTS**
>
> Create a spot on your bulletin board, Web site or blog where students regularly seek out and review their favorite, or most useful, podcasts. Decide in advance on criteria for review (See chapter 3) and a rating system.

Podcasts are a great way to promote activities in your school to students, parents and community. Podcast newscasts or recordings from live events (band concerts, media fairs, quiz bowl events, and so on) are compelling content that can be archived and enjoyed for a long time.

PODCASTS AS RESEARCH TOOLS

You already know that your students are getting really good at "googling for gaps"—that is, searching the Internet for gaps in their research for papers and projects for your classroom. Podcasts can provide an additional resource for research and study.

Three activities immediately pop up when most think of using podcasts to assist student research:

1. **Collecting podcast addresses or resources around a specific area of study:** Challenge students, for example, to search and collect podcasts related to oral history, or the language and culture of a specific country. Develop a form or template for reporting their findings on a class Web site, e-book, or blog.

2. **Creating your own directory of resources:** Later in this book you'll find lots of podcast resources sorted by curriculum area, and a list of podcast directories on the Internet in the appendix. Sometimes, though, it makes sense to create your own directory—perhaps they are "safe" (non-explicit or teacher-approved) or perhaps just a paring down of the thousands of podcasts available. Post the directory to the school Web site or blog and share your learning with others.

3. **Listening to podcasts and taking notes:** Many teachers find that students will spend much more time listening to podcasts for research than they would searching more traditional media like print. Not only does this type of research breed better listening skills, but the added dimension of listening to the spoken word, or in the case of a vodcast, watching a video, often nets a deeper understanding of the areas of study.

SHARING NEWS AND INFORMATION

There was a time when a student would visit the front office early each school day to retrieve a stack of freshly blue-inked mimeographed pages which they would dutifully deliver to every classroom. The teacher would then read the daily announcements to often blank and mostly foggy faces. Fast-forward a few years and closed-circuit television delivers fast-paced, student-created newscasts that capture the attention of students (and adults). The next sea-change happens when these newscasts can be shared easily with the school's community. Now, many schools offer podcasts of news and events on their Web sites. Parents and students can subscribe and when the students arrive at school, the day's news is ready for transfer to their iPod. Their parents can listen to (or view) the podcasts online, or download them to their own digital music player.

PROFESSIONAL DEVELOPMENT

Couldn't get to your favorite educational conference or event? Chances are growing that you'll be able to find a podcast of the proceedings online. Educators everywhere are embracing podcasts as a way to extend the reach of their conference presentations. The larger educational conferences, such as NECC (National Educational Computing Conference) and FETC (Florida Educational Technology Conference) all offer podcasts of selected workshops and events. While it's no substitute for being there and soaking up the atmosphere, collaborating with others and browsing the latest technologies, these event-driven podcasts are a terrific way to increase your knowledge of what's new or what's happening in your area of study.

It's not just events that are podcast, of course. Schools like Lesley College in Massachusetts offer podcasts for preservice and inservice teachers on a wide variety of subjects. Check out the Higher Education podcasts in chapter 15 for some samples.

ARCHIVING LECTURES

A visitor from another planet who landed on just about any college or university campus might think that the strange bipedal creatures walking around were born with the ubiquitous white earplugs dangling from their ears. It's hard nowadays not to see students dashing from class to class with their iPod strapped to their shoulder, hidden in their backpack, or stuffed in a belt holster.

College students, it turns out, are listening to more than just the latest tunes from No Doubt or the Black Eyed Peas. They're just as likely to be listening to Chemistry 101 or reviewing German grammar. That's because the number of higher education instructors who record, then archive, their lectures for later download as a podcast is growing like kudzu (the relentless Japanese vine that grows an amazing 12 inches per *day*—also referred to as "the plant that ate the South").

Podcast lectures are also a boon for students at any level who miss class because they are ill or just need to review the content because their instructor speaks faster than their brain wants to work.

FIELD RECORDING

In this increasingly wireless world, some podcasters are taking their podcasts on the road. Using smartphones or WiFi access, you can record a podcast just about anywhere and then upload it to your blog or podcast server and share activities and experiences from remote locations.

The ability to record audio right into your iPod (www.belkin.com) also allows for excellent field note-taking. Now students can share observations while they're still in the field. Interviews and virtual tours can make for a very compelling listening experience.

STUDY SUPPORT

One of the great things about podcasts is that they are digital. That means you can listen over and over again to increase comprehension. Students are finding that repetitively listening to podcast lectures helps them focus on critical material. Creating study podcasts to share with students is also becoming more popular, especially in law or medical schools where students are faced with the daunting challenge of cramming huge amounts of information into their brains in an incredibly short time.

> ## » TIP
>
> **TRY VIDEO**
>
> Vodcasting, or podcasts with video, is still relatively new—as are the devices capable of playing them—but that doesn't mean you and your students shouldn't dip your toes into the waters and give it a try. The production takes far more time, because you have to worry about the visual element and some content can't be presented visually, but often it's worth the effort. Try to avoid the "two students in front of the school banner" syndrome. That works for daily announcements in your school, but it might not be of sufficient production value to keep the community at large glued to their iPods.

PRODUCING PODCASTS

Once your students get used to listening to podcasts, it won't be long until they'll want to create their own. Students get excited about creating podcasts because it gives them a way to share their work with a wider audience. Their podcasts can be placed in online directories (such as iTunes Podcast Directory) alongside podcasts by their favorite rock star or newsperson.

As with other new technologies, podcast creation often serves to kickstart even reluctant learners into meaningful activities. Your students *will* get excited. This added motivation often turns into a competition for the best podcast—an effect that you can use to even further motivate students.

GETTING STARTED

In chapter 1, you'll find a starter list of what you need to listen to or create your own podcasts. In general, most teachers begin podcasting by exploring the tools. Figuring out how things work—and getting a picture of the workflow, if you will—is a good place to start. Listening to podcasts from other schools or from professional podcasters is a great way to begin as well.

Once you've become comfortable with the process of listening to or creating podcasts, introduce it to your students. You can begin using a big screen or smartboard to display a Web site or blog containing podcast content and playing a few examples. Then talk with students about how this content can be made more mobile by transferring the files to music players (iPods, cell phones, etc.).

Next you can open a discussion about how to determine whether a podcast meets your needs, is credible, and has a high enough production value so as not to get in the way of conveying the message. Chapter 3 has some starter rubrics.

Podcasting and Curriculum Standards

You'll find that podcasting fits nicely as a tool for meeting a variety of standards, both state and national. Since the process of listening to, or planning and creating, a podcast involves communication, any standards dealing with reading, writing, listening, and speaking are very appropriately met with the podcast activities.

Cross-curricular goals are easily met with podcasting projects too, as demonstrated in the following lesson. Here, students create a newscast about what will happen in an ongoing issue or conflict *tomorrow*, addressing three sets of standards in the process.

MODEL LESSON

Telling Tomorrow's Story Today

Here's an example of a teacher-tested activity that uses podcasts both as a resource and as a final product. It's a long lesson that could be broken up into segments, or selected segments used independently. You can use the overall structure of the lesson as a template for just about any lesson you dream up.

Description

Students choose a current event or issue and conduct research using the Web, including podcasts, to create their own podcast featuring their conclusions about how the story might unfold within the next week.

Subject	Language Arts, Journalism, Communications, Social Studies
Grade Level	Grades 6–12, Higher Education
Time	Six class periods (approximate)

Objectives

Students will:

> participate in a class discussion about key political, social, or newsworthy issues

> collect, analyze, and present background research and information on a selected issue

> use podcasts and other electronic media to gather key information and content

> produce a podcast-newscast written in present tense, presenting "tomorrow's news" on their chosen issue

Standards

NETS•S Grade 9–12
Performance Indicators   1, 2, 5, 7, 8, 9

English Language Arts Standards   1, 2, 3, 4, 5, 6, 7, 8, 11, 12

Social Studies Standards   II, III, VII, VII, IX, X

Tools and Resources

Software   word processing, sound editing, Web publishing

Hardware   computer, microphone, Internet connection

Activities

Invite the class to brainstorm a list of current social, political or newsworthy issues that are in the news on the day of the discussion. Jot the ideas on the whiteboard.

Have students work in groups of three or four to choose one of the issues, then have them search the Web for news and background necessary to create a one-page current issue brief on the topic. This brief should contain a complete description of current events surrounding or related to the issue at hand.

Ask groups to comb the Web for podcasts from news organizations, or other sources, that mention or expand on the chosen issue. Once they've found the podcast and screened it to ensure that it's appropriate for classroom use, have them play a segment for the rest of the class and discuss the credibility of the source. Add information from the podcast to the issue brief.

Have students work independently to write a short news item with their forecast of how the story might unfold in a week's time. If they're writing about a war or military conflict, for example, they should use research and information from the podcast to predict, in as much detail as they can, how the conflict will unfold, what changes might occur and the reasons why those conflicts continued as they predict. Update briefs should be written in present tense and in newscast format.

Challenge students to reconvene their groups and produce a short "tomorrow's news" podcast for presentation to the class. You'll need to allow time for planning and recording the podcast, post-production (see chapter 1), and polishing.

On presentation day, ask students to share the "today" podcast and selected excerpts from other research, and then present their own podcast for "tomorrow's news."

Assessment

Each part of the activity could be assessed using individual rubrics focusing on the quality of research and the technical and content aspects of the student-produced podcast.

If you're a technology coordinator or an early adopter of podcasting for your school, you might assemble a list of relevant state standards and distribute them to teachers as a guideline for planning their lessons. This kind of list also helps educators not familiar with the possibilities of podcasting dip their toes in the water safely, knowing that the activities they're likely to create are viable alternatives to other, more traditional, teaching and learning methods.

Managing Podcasts in the Classroom

Podcasting will be quite popular once you introduce it to your students. You'll find that one of the biggest challenges is classroom management. You have lots of students who need access to the tools to create or listen to podcasts, and very little time to do it.

Sound familiar? These are some of the same challenges we have with other classroom resources. The best way around the challenges is to meet them head-on using schedules for accessing the equipment, finding sneaky ways to purchase more computers and audio equipment for making podcasts, and developing quick-start manuals (something your students can help with) to guide new users through the process of listening to, or creating, podcasts.

SCHEDULING

Because podcasts are found on the Web, it's a good idea to think ahead about the process of scheduling time for students to download their podcasts for later use in the classroom. Generally, downloading to their desktop first, then to a mobile device, like a handheld, smartphone or music player (like an Apple iPod), is the easiest way to manage the workflow. Consider allocating download time or listening time (if you don't want to store the podcast locally) at the beginning of class, or rotate groups through the listening stations. If they have their own listening device, like an iPod, then students can listen at their desk when the appropriate point in the lesson arrives.

If your students are creating podcasts, you should schedule time for planning and script/talking-point writing, time for the actual recording, and time for post-production (adding theme music, editing content, etc.). In general, it'll take about 1/3 of the time allotted for planning and 2/3 for recording and post-production.

In the case of vodcasts, things get decidedly trickier as you'll be juggling video equipment, props, scenery, etc. Set aside one or more computer stations in your classroom or lab for student editing bays. Vodcast production takes two to three times longer than audio podcast production.

SNEAKY WAYS TO GET FUNDING

Although podcasting is a technology, it's not a piece of hardware. You will, however, need hardware to play and/or create your own podcasts. There are many grants, including those from the Bill & Melinda Gates Educational Foundation, the George Lucas Foundation, and others, that allow for grants relating to multimedia production and use in the classroom. When you write grants for podcasting, focus on the innovative use of technology to do new things—not just taking an old plan and adding a podcast. Projects that teach others, provide increased accessibility, and foster the use of new technologies still get the most attention.

Another sneaky way to fund the use or production of podcasts is to think of the technology as a media resource. Because podcasts are multimedia, just like videos, DVDs, cassette tapes, and (ugh) film-strips—they're a media resource. They can be archived and cataloged. Sometimes media specialists or district media coordinators have funds that can be used to purchase microphones and other recording equipment and software you might need for the production of podcasts. It's worth a try.

QUICK-START MANUALS

Arthur C. Clarke once said, "Any sufficiently advanced technology is indistinguishable from magic." (*Profiles of The Future*, 1961) and to many people, podcasting seems like magic. It turns out, like most technologies useful in the classroom, that if you know the right things about the task at hand, it's easier to do than you think. That's true for podcasting too.

One way to streamline the process of educating others is to create a quick-start manual. This manual is a two- or three-page document that shows, step by step, what to do to listen to, or create, a podcast. You can look back at chapter 1 of this book and create your own, or surf the Web for snippets and patch one together. However you proceed, don't get bogged down in the myriad of technical possibilities for audio and video production. Focus on the basics, reminding the learner all the while that the *content* is the most important element of any podcast—production comes after that.

PODCAST DILEMMA: STORING AND ORGANIZING CONTENT

Stanford University now has more than 1,000 hours of podcast content online. The University of Missouri has a huge library of lectures and sporting events and encourages students to upload work for review. It probably won't take long before your servers get stuffed with podcasts—particularly if you're sharing vodcast content. The question becomes, do you purchase a bunch of servers and create your own library, or do you rely on a third party?

One solution is an innovative program from Apple called iTunes U. The program offers customized pages through Apple's (free) iTunes software. The University of Missouri, University of Wisconsin-Madison, the University of Michigan's School of Dentistry and California's Stanford University all allow faculty and students to upload and share information to their customized iTunes portal. The portals are typically customized with school colors, logos and photography and offer integrated podcasting support and archiving. For more information visit www.apple.com/education/solutions/itunes_u/.

Others have chosen to build their own libraries on servers in their data centers or central offices.

Other Resources

The possibilities are endless for using podcasts to support instruction. There are many, many more ideas than I've listed above and most of them are available through an easy search of the Internet.

CHAPTER 3

Evaluating Podcasts for Classroom Use

A s with any content you and your students find on the Web, some podcasts are more useful and appropriate for your classroom than others. It makes sense to give some thought to how you and your students will make that distinction and how you'll evaluate podcasts created by your class.

This chapter presents several ideas for examining and evaluating podcasts across the curriculum, including some teacher-tested rubrics. Based on experience, the process of reviewing podcasts can be educational, and a lot of fun.

Choosing the Right Podcasts for Your Classroom

Every evening in most major markets there are more than 200 television shows airing on different regular and cable channels at one time. As anyone with a remote will tell you, often you surf through the channels and find that there's "nothing on." Either the content isn't compelling, or, more often, what's offered is of low quality.

Evaluating podcasts created by your students or by others is not an exact science. Besides looking at overall content and production value, things like the source are important too.

Even though we've taken steps to qualify the podcasts in this book, as with any resource that enters your classroom, you'll want to screen and evaluate the content to make sure it meets school and community standards before recommending or using the podcast in your classroom. Since creating a podcast is easy, and the Nintendo generation loves to explore, you'll find a sizeable (and growing) number of podcasts that probably are not appropriate for classroom use. Many young (and older) folks are using podcasts as audio or video blogs (Web logs) that chronicle their lives or offer opportunities to express opinions. It is very important that you screen any podcast, but especially those created and served up as blogs. Like surfing the Web for other content, you just never know what might pop up in a podcast blog.

Top 10 questions to ask as you evaluate podcasts for classroom use:

1. Is the content appropriate for your current area of study?

Back in the days when desktop computers were introduced into schools, we often felt compelled to use the technology because so many taxpayer resources went into funding them. There was sometimes a notion that if we didn't use computers every day or provide equity of access across the school that we weren't justifying the investment. In so many cases we trotted the class down to the computer lab "because it was Tuesday" and not because it necessarily fit well into what we were teaching at the time. Kids left language arts classes to "do spreadsheets" or we scheduled seat time in the lab to appease a watchful PTA. OK. Not everyone really did that, but some of us did because we understood both the power and limitations of computer technology in schools.

With podcasts it's kind of the same process. We'll be tempted to grab podcasts off the Web or assign students to search out podcasts because everyone's talking about them and so they must be good. The reality is that podcasts are more like resource materials, or, if you're teaching how to make a

> ## » TIP
>
> **EXAMPLE PODCASTS**
>
> Grab two or three examples of exemplary podcasts and burn them to a CD to distribute to other teachers in your school or district. You might also corral other teachers in your subject area and develop lesson plans that logically integrate podcasts.

podcast, an exercise in technology awareness and skill building. When you browse the podcasts in this book, make sure to think about how appropriate the content in that podcast is for the knowledge needs and grade level of your students.

2. Does the podcast add to or enhance your current lesson plan?

As with any resource, you'll find that podcast content can be an excellent way to turbocharge many activities. If you're a foreign language teacher, for example, you're highly likely to find a good quality audio or video podcast in your language of choice—perfect for students to use to learn, hone, or review skills. Of course, the trick is to listen to the podcast yourself first and direct the learner toward a goal (some way to demonstrate learning).

3. Does the content and production of the podcast meet school and community standards for acceptable use in your school?

Freedom of speech is a wonderful and treasured thing. You'll find examples of people speaking their mind all over the Web in the form of all kinds of digital content. Many people have discovered that they'd rather speak their mind than type their minds and are launching diaries, blogs, and diatribes in the form of podcasts in record numbers. That means, of course, that you're likely to be able to find and listen to or view just about anything you can imagine (and many things you couldn't imagine) as podcasts. It usually takes about 45 seconds to determine if something just doesn't feel right for your classroom. Content might be littered with expletives, present ideas uncomfortable or inappropriate for your school or just content that's non-factual.

> **» | TIP**
>
> **DEVELOP A CHECKLIST**
>
> Check out chapter 3 and work with your students to develop a checklist for evaluating the content and appropriateness of podcasts to be used in your classroom. Post the final checklist on your school's Web site or find other ways to share it with others.

There's also the need to watch for the production value of the podcast. If the audio or video is garbled, the speaker speaks too quickly, the volume is impossibly low, there's background noise that distracts or other annoyances, it's probably a good clue that you should move on to select another podcast resource. Not to say that all useful podcasts are jazzy Hollywood productions with professional intro music and syrupy-voiced hosts. Some of the best podcasts I've heard were very simply presented.

A word to the wise is to carefully evaluate the source, credibility, content and presentation of a podcast or podcast provider before you assign the podcast as required or optional listening.

4. Is the content of the podcast well organized and easy to follow?

A good Web site offers content that is logically organized and always lets the site visitor know where they are in the site structure. Like great Web sites, the best examples of podcasts offer digital signposts such as a specific introduction announcing the topic, date, audience and other information and, in the case of a longer podcast (an hour), several "you're listening to a podcast from ABC Elementary School, Anywhere, USA" breaks. In addition, if your podcast is over about 15 minutes long, you should probably subdivide your content into logical units and provide an audio table of contents to kick things off.

If you're evaluating rather than creating podcasts, listen for those "digital signposts" and for rambling content. Think about how audio books are presented (if you've not tried audio books, you're missing something—visit www.audible.com for some free and commercial titles) and try to choose podcasts that employ some of the same organizational methods (chapters, outlines, etc.).

5. Is the content of the podcast compelling enough to hold the attention of your audience?

It's no secret that the attention span of our students, just like most of us, seems to be decreasing with time. In this age of immediate information gratification, we're not used to waiting for anything and we're not likely to tolerate material that we think is boring. Like most other audio or video media, podcasts span the continuum from can't get enough to deadly boring. It's a highly subjective evaluation of course, since something you consider boring might be positively addictive for others. A general rule of thumb is to listen to the podcast and balance your evaluation between the importance of the content and the delivery. Every educational podcast, like every education film, won't be Top Gun but at least you can toss the ones that drone on more like the teacher in Ferris Bueller's Day Off... "anyone, anyone?"

6. Is the podcast in a digital format that works for your classroom?

Most of the downloadable podcasts are MP3 files, the same kind of files you're used to downloading for your iPod or other MP3 player. There are podcasts that are in other formats such as MOV (QuickTime), MPEG or even AVI. MP3 files are most compatible with the largest number of desktop and mobile devices, and the tools used to create, edit and share podcasts. Stick with MP3 as a format and you should have an easier introduction to podcasting.

7. Was the podcast produced by a source you consider credible?

Because you're using (assigning?) podcasts as a replacement or enhancement of other classroom curriculum resources, it is your role to ensure that the content presented is factual and aligned to your classroom and district's goals and objectives, meets curriculum standards, and that the information doesn't confuse (or enrage) learners.

Just like any article you research in the library or download from the Web, you should always consider the source when selecting a podcast. Tried and true sources like the NEA, CSPAN, CNN, and the Discovery Channel are probably safer than "Todd's podcast." That's not to say that "Todd's podcast" isn't good and factual, it's just a caveat emptor situation. You can assess the credibility of the source by looking at the hosting site (the place you go to actually download the podcast), the author, the group backing the podcast, and the resources cited during the podcast if the podcast is instructional in nature.

8. Is listening to the podcast the best method of learning about this topic for your students?

As an educator you have the wonderful option of many different ways to convey information. We use video, the Web, textbooks, and even (gasp!) paper handouts. Podcasts, presented in the proper context in a learning environment, are a great way to deliver information, especially for auditory (or visual if it's a video podcast) learners. The ability to stop, start and replay also makes for a tool appropriate for students with special learning needs or challenges—as well as everyone else who wishes to learn by repetition. As you listen to and review podcasts for use in your classroom, take special care to think about all the tools available and resist the "just because it's cool" temptation. Podcasts can enrich the learning environment—when they are selected as the right tool for the right job.

9. Is the podcast supported by additional online content (a Web site with further resources or archives, for example)?

As podcasting takes hold on the Net, you'll find more and more examples of content-rich Web sites that provide more information about the content you hear in a podcast. In other cases, the Web site gives basic information and the podcast gives you the "advanced" content.

Many sites, especially those hosting education-related podcasts, offer rich libraries of print and multimedia content that provide opportunities to broaden learning.

10. Does the podcast include any usage rights that limit the broadcast or distribution of content?

Like radio and TV, podcast content is subject to digital rights management. While the majority of podcasts are distributed as "freeware" (free subscription), some media outlets and professional content providers are beginning to offer podcast content as a paid subscription. That means, of course, that it's up to you to police the use and distribution of that content. Check the hosting Web site to see if there are any restrictions beyond fair use that might dictate what you do with the podcast content.

If you or your students create your own podcasts and wish to establish usage rights, check out Creative Commons (http://creativecommons.org/podcasting/) for a free option for tagging your podcasts to legally protect content. This site offers a set of common sense rules for sharing content (music, blog info, podcasts).

Rubrics for Podcast Evaluation

Evaluating podcasts as curriculum materials is different from evaluating the content from podcasts brought into the classroom. Most find that, like many other more creative endeavors in the schools, it's better to use a rubric created by you or your students to assess podcast projects.

There are obviously many elements to a podcast, but what follows are three teacher-tested favorites for evaluating podcast content. These rubrics focus on general content, technical content, and related skills.

Here are a couple of rubrics you can use to evaluate podcasts created by students or teachers. The rubrics below are a compendium of the 40 or so rubrics submitted or researched for the publication of this book. They each offer a different perspective but are designed to be highly customizable, so don't be afraid to excerpt these or make your own from scratch.

RUBRIC ONE: Focus on content and execution. Easy to understand.

CATEGORY	Excellent	Good	Fair	Needs Improvement
Content	Demonstrates a full understanding of the topic.	Demonstrates a good understanding of the topic.	Demonstrates a good understanding of some of the topic.	Does not show understanding of the topic.
Music Intro/Exit	Music is present, creative, and appropriate for all listeners. Intro/exit provided good signposts for listening.	Music is present, with some creativity and appropriate for most listeners. Intro/exit material present, but not effective.	Music is present, but is not appropriate for the tone or content of the podcast. Intro/exit material not present.	No music or intro/exit material present.
Presentation	Interesting, well-rehearsed, compelling delivery, grammatically correct, paced well.	Relatively interesting, rehearsed, good grammar.	Choppy delivery, errors in grammar, contents not very compelling.	Delivery needs improvement. Grammar needs improvement. Content not compelling.
Audio or Video	Clean and without distraction or extraneous noise.	Acceptable, but with noticeable background noise or other distractions.	Background noise or other distractions excessive, overall audio below average.	Quality unacceptable.

RUBRIC TWO: Focus on technical aspects, then content. More specific and probably more acceptable to experienced podcasters.

CATEGORY	Excellent	Good	Fair	Needs Improvement
Technical	Audio clear and error-free. Music and sound effects used correctly and appropriately. RSS feed works.	Audio contains few errors or is not clear. Music used but not very effectively. RSS feed information incomplete.	Audio errors prevalent. Music detracted from understanding of the content. RSS feed didn't work.	Audio errors interfered with understanding or comprehension. Music not present or used inappropriately. No RSS feed.
Content	Demonstrates a full understanding of the topic. Content is clear and correct.	Demonstrates a good understanding of the topic.	Demonstrates a good understanding of some of the topic.	Does not show understanding of the topic.
Organization	Clear outline of content for the podcast complete with resources necessary to do the job.	Outline offers a glimpse of content but is not complete.	Outline doesn't clearly express the content or organization of the podcast.	Outline doesn't really reflect the content or organization needed.

PART TWO

Podcast Directory

PUTTING TOGETHER a podcast directory is great fun, even though it's also hard work. For me, searching for the "best" sites became an obsession. There are thousands of podcasts out there and choosing the right ones for this book wasn't easy. Some of these sites were chosen based on the evaluation strategies presented in chapter 3, some were suggested by fellow educators, some by students, some were just stumbled upon while browsing the Web.

What you won't see in the directory are very many examples of personal blogs (Web logs) or "edutainment" sites. The personal blogs come and go too often, even though many offer really excellent perspectives on teaching and learning.

The edutainment (education + entertainment) sites, such as those published by commercial entities like theme parks and department stores, may have value, but they're not really in the top tier of useful things for your classroom. If you're interested in those genres, launch iTunes or your favorite browser and browse the Net for them. They're easy to find.

Podcasts, like other content available on the Internet, can appear or disappear in a flash. Podcasts may move to other servers, change formats or titles, or just disappear without a trace. All the podcasts in this book were checked before the directory was published, but I'm not naïve enough to think every one will be around by the time this book hits the shelves. If you try a podcast and get a dead-end, here are some recommendations:

> Use a search engine or access iTunes podcast directory and search for the title of the podcast, or the originator (ABC Elementary, Discovery Channel, etc.).

> Check to make sure you've correctly typed the podcast site's URL. URLs for the actual podcast (as opposed to the site hosting the podcast) tend to be long and accuracy counts (check case, special characters, etc.).

> Wait. Sometimes podcasts are so popular that the machines serving up the content are overwhelmed. Try again in about 5 minutes.

While most modern browsers, such as Firefox, Internet Explorer 7.0, and Safari, have integrated support for RSS feeds, older browsers might not. Make sure you check to see if there's a more current version of your browser available if you have trouble with the links in this book. Alternatively, you can use desktop feed-readers like Feed Demon or Newsgator.

Web feeds, like those in RSS or Atom format, are usually linked to the word "subscribe" or one of the following three icons, which are most often orange. The square icon is the standard.

All that said, enjoy the directory. If you have suggestions for podcasts to include in later editions or updates, please email me at bard@techthree.com.

CHAPTER 4

Podcasts for General Education and Administration

A collection of podcast content about teaching and learning

Since many of the most prolific podcasters are educators in colleges, universities and technical schools, there is no shortage of content about the art and science of education. You'll find podcasts that talk about everything from the latest techniques for discipline management to school safety. You're very likely to find podcasts of sessions from your favorite educational conference too. And, you'll find many sites dedicated to building skills in teaching and background on the philosophies behind those skills.

Conversations in Education

www.hamline.edu/gse/conversations/

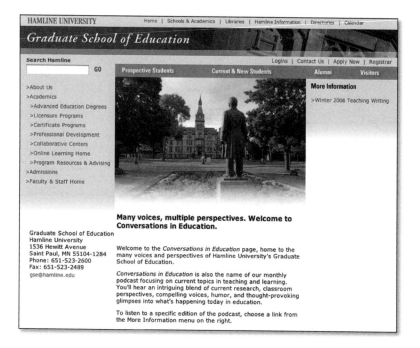

Description

Conversations in Education is a podcast on current educational topics from Hamline University. Each show focuses on a current topic related to teaching and learning, and brings you a collection of stories exploring that theme. The podcasts feature a wide spectrum of education-relevant content including research, interviews, and on-the-scene looks at what's happening in today's classroom.

Sample topics

> Student Interactive Systems

> Understanding by Design

> Teaching Writing with Students of All Ages

Classroom Applications

There are many examples of Colleges of Education that offer podcast content. Hamline sets itself apart because it's relatively consistent in delivering content that both holds your attention and offers useful tips and content ideal for preservice or inservice educators. The school also follows a standard format, an opening, outline of the content of the podcast, podcast content, then a review. This is a good model to follow for your own podcasts.

Details

Audience	K–12 educators, higher education educators, preservice teachers
Type	audio
Resource type	instructional, blog
Frequency	monthly
Source/Author	Hamline University Graduate School of Education
Location	Saint Paul, MN
Source URL	www.hamline.edu

Learning.com Podcasts

www.learning.com/podcast/

Description

Learning.com offers a variety of podcasts featuring nuggets of wisdom from Alan November, a recognized leader in education technology. Most of the podcasts are recordings from Alan's presentations at national education conferences and events. Topics range from issues and trends in education to cutting-edge technologies and their impact on teaching and learning.

Sample Topics

> › Alan November at CUE, Palm Springs, CA; presenting Building Knowledge without Boundaries, Bringing 21st Century Skills into the Classroom.

> › Alan November at San Mateo, CA; presenting Integrating Technology with Math and Reading.

Classroom Applications

Alan November remains a favorite among speakers on the education circuit presenting pithy content scattered with both wit and wisdom. The podcasts can serve as discussion starters for professional development in educational technology, or as a research touch-point for technology planners in schools and districts. Check out Learning.com's monthly newsletter for a heads-up on upcoming topics.

Details

Audience	K–12 educators, higher education educators, preservice teachers
Type	audio
Resource type	instructional
Frequency	special
Source/Author	Alan November
Source URL	www.learning.com

Teaching for the Future

www.teachingforthefuture.com

Description

Teaching for the Future is a nicely polished education podcast about implementing media and technology literacy. It is presented by an artist from New Jersey who now lives in Cambridge, Massachusetts and is a grad student at Lesley University. Dave LaMorte talks about the importance of media literacy and educational technology in the classroom and how it can change education forever.

Sample topics

> I Am a Level 4 Educator

> Our Country, Our Truck?

> Art-bots for Kids, Burger Kong, and Video Game Pedagogy

> Alive in Baghdad

> Constitutionally Speaking

Classroom Applications

Animated presenter Dave LaMorte presents a fresh perspective on major trends and issues in education. In contrast to the more entrenched education speakers, LaMorte offers a more gut-level response to often controversial topics such as open classrooms and 21st-century learning. He often cites blogs and Web sites containing research and background for discussion and isn't afraid to speak his mind about what he thinks about the issues. The site will provoke both discussion and, probably, argument. You might recommend staff listen to the podcasts prior to discussions in faculty meetings, or professional development activities. It's an excellent example of a podcast produced for the good of the masses by an energetic college student.

Details

Audience	K–12 educators, higher education educators, preservice teachers
Type	audio
Resource type	instructional, blog
Frequency	varies
Source/Author	Dave LaMorte
Source URL	www.teachingforthefuture.com

ASCD Talks With an Author

www.ascd.org/portal/site/ascd/menuitem.0f78fd8115519c05414
4aa33e3108a0c/

Description

The Association for Curriculum and Development (ASCD) interviews authors of ASCD-published works. These thought-provoking interviews present a unique author's perspective on the content and creation of their work, expanding on topics presented in works for sale by ASCD. As with the ASCD library, topics vary from pedagogy to research, with a scattering of trend and issue information to spice things up.

Sample Topics

> Jane Hill and Kathleen Flynn—Classroom Instruction That Works with English Language Learners

> Alfie Kohn—Beyond Discipline: From Compliance to Community

> Mike Schmoker—Results Now

Classroom Applications

It doesn't really matter if you've read these author's books before you hear the podcasts. Often they share just enough information to get you interested, so don't be surprised if you want to know more. The podcasts are well constructed and organized, with excellent sound quality, and could be a good way for preservice and inservice educators to keep up with issues in research and teaching. The site offers streaming audio in QuickTime, RealPlayer and Windows Media Player formats.

Details

Audience	K–12 educators, higher education educators, preservice teachers
Type	audio
Resource type	instructional
Frequency	varies
Source/Author	ASCD
Source URL	www.ascd.org

Parents.com Parents Podcast

Link to podcast through iTunes:
**http://phobos.apple.com/WebObjects/MZStore.woa/wa/
viewPodcast?id=171486217**

Link to podcast through Parents.com:
**www.parents.com/parents/category.jhtml?categoryid=/
templatedata/parents/category/data/1153764208601.xml**

Description

A presentation of expert advice and counsel from the editors of *Parents* magazine. Very slickly produced, these podcasts offer practical tips and techniques perfect for parents and teachers who deal with basic behavioral, emotional and intellectual issues like childhood obesity and attention deficit disorder. The archived podcasts suggest that the magazine produces new content about every two months.

Sample Topics

> Sibling Rivalry

> Overweight Kids

> Back to School

Classroom Applications

Counselors and PTA members will find these podcasts informative and helpful. The programs flow nicely and are likely to stimulate discussion and questions about the issues presented. In the Overweight Kids segment, for example, you get a perspective from the parent of an overweight teen, the teenager, and a dietitian—all of whom provide good insight into a very relevant issue.

Details

Audience	educators, parents
Type	audio
Resource type	instructional
Frequency	varies
Source/Author	Parents Magazine editors
Source URL	www.parents.com

The Center for Comprehensive School Reform and Improvement

www.centerforcsri.org/index.php?option=
com_content&task=view&id=153&Itemid=84

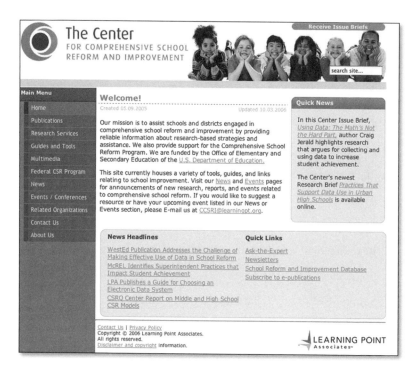

Description

These podcasts, presented in conjunction with the North Central Regional Educational Laboratory (NCREL), offer discussion and insight about improving learning through the use of validated evidence. The podcasts are supported with extensive research and documentation available on the CSRI Web site.

Sample Topics

> An Introduction to Basing Our Practice on Better Evidence

> Changing the Nature of the Education Conversation

> Trends in Using Measurement to Improve Learning

Classroom Applications

If you want in-depth discussion, background, and perspectives on educational issues, these podcasts are a good place to begin. Podcasts will no doubt pose as many questions as are answered and you will likely jump from agreement to disagreement many times during each session. Professional development classes featuring discussion on trends in education, particularly the practice of teaching and learning, are a likely place for these podcasts to be used. The Web site offers excellent background and information about speakers and topics covered—extending the podcast experience well beyond the audio content.

Details

Audience	K–12 and higher education educators
Type	audio
Resource type	instructional
Frequency	varies
Source/Author	CCSRI
Location	Washington, D.C.
Source URL	www.centerforcsri.org

Learning Matters: The Merrow Report

www.pbs.org/merrow/podcast/

Description

K–12 and Higher Ed issues presented by John Merrow, a veteran education reporter for *The NewsHour* on PBS. Segments run from hard-hitting reports to perspectives presented by political pundits presented in a news-like and very polished format.

Sample Topics

> Measuring Learning

> The Weighted Student Formula Debate

> Preparing for Standardized Tests

> Frustrations and Accomplishments

Classroom Applications

I chose this podcast because the perspective on educational trends and issues comes from a reporter, not an educator. As a result, you'll find a high-level analysis of issues such as standardized testing, supported by interviews and research, but without the educator's perspective. Contrast this content with that presented by NCREL (see directory entry earlier in this chapter) for an interesting discussion-starter. These podcasts are perfect for your commute to or from school and will likely make for interesting lunchtime conversation.

Details

Audience	K–12 and higher education educators
Type	audio
Resource type	instructional, blog
Frequency	varies
Source/Author	John Merrow, Learning Matters, Inc.
Source URL	www.pbs.org/merrow/

Coming of Age: An Introduction to the New Worldwide Web

http://comingofage.podomatic.com

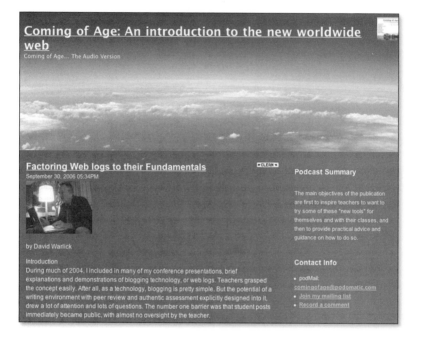

Description

A podcast series based on the popular book of the same name. These podcasts provide a set of stories, presented by leaders in education and technology, describing how Web 2.0 technology can be used in schools, including the use of technology in support of learning and fostering individualized curriculum.

Sample Presenters

> Miles Berry

> John Bidder

> Mechelle de Craene

> David Warlick

> Shawn Wheeler

> Alan November

Classroom Applications

Both the book (*Coming of Age,* edited by Terry Freedman) and these podcasts will inspire readers to research and explore the next generation of Web tools and technologies. The credibility of presentations is high and the discussion interesting and thought-provoking. I'd recommend reading and listening to this content before technology professional development activities or before attending educational conferences. Be sure to check out the supporting Web site for ideas about interesting blogs to read.

Details

Audience	K–12 and higher education educators
Type	audio
Resource type	instructional audio book
Frequency	varies
Source/Author	Shawn Wheeler
Location	varies
Source URL	http://comingofage.podomatic.com

Intelligenic KidCast: Podcasting in the Classroom

www.intelligenic.com/blog/?feed=rss2

Description

KidCast is the offspring of a professional development course focused on introducing students and teachers to podcasting. The experience netted the podcast, as well as a book entitled *KidCast: Podcasting in the Classroom*, and a Web site rich in content about introducing podcasting to your students, administrators and fellow teachers.

Sample Topics

› Talking to Administrators about Podcasting

› Sound Seeing Tours

› Where in the World?

Classroom Applications

Dan Schmit offers an educator's real-world perspective about podcasting. He's easy to listen to and his content is succinct and relevant. Several of the podcasts on the site are archives of his conference presentations that provide an excellent overview to podcasting in education. Content on the Web site (a blog) supports the presentations and offers excellent source material for presentations you might create about these emerging technologies. The content on this site is perfect for technology coordinators or professional developers who need background for introductory classes or presentations.

Details

Audience	K–12 and higher education educators
Type	audio
Resource type	informational, blog
Frequency	weekly
Source/Author	Dan Schmit
Location	Salinas, CA
Source URL	www.intelligenic.com

Learning and Teaching Scotland

www.ltscotland.org.uk/rss/settpodcasts.xml

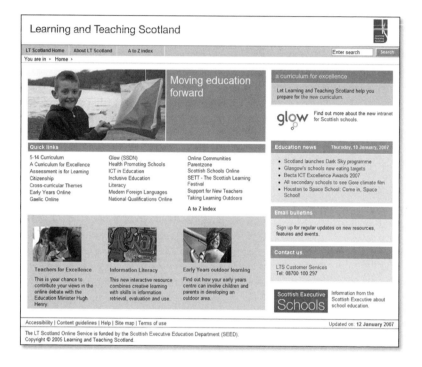

Description

Learning and Teaching Scotland is an organization dedicated to the development and support of the Scottish curriculum. LT Scotland works with the Scottish Executive and Education authorities to provide insight and guidance in moving forward the national education improvement agenda. The podcasts primarily highlight seminars from SETT 2005 and 2006—the Scottish Learning Festival (www.settshow.com).

Sample Topics

> The Powerful Effects of Teaching Thinking Explicitly as a Skill

> Turning Good Teachers into Great Leaders

> Cross-continental, Cross-cutting Themes

Classroom Applications

I like this podcast series because it gives a bit of worldly perspective to teaching and illustrates other education entities that lead the way in technology in the classroom and curriculum. The podcasts were recorded at workshops delivered at Scotland's largest education technology conference and offer very high quality content and perspective that will energize technology planners and inservice educators.

Details

Audience	K–12 and higher education educators
Type	audio
Resource type	instructional, informational
Frequency	special event
Source/Author	Learning and Teaching in Scotland
Location	Glasgow, Scotland
Source URL	www.ltscotland.org.uk

Minneapolis Public Schools

www.mpls.k12.mn.us/mpsboard.html

Description

Minneapolis Public Schools was one of the first education organizations to offer broadcasts of school board meetings in audio format. The meetings are archived on the site and provide an intriguing look into a district with more than 40,000 students. The broadcasts are unedited and presented in their entirety.

Sample Topics

> Special Discussion Meeting

> Regular Meeting

Classroom Applications

I included this audio series because it's a fine example of how school boards are jumping on the podcast bandwagon. The district uses podcasts to share meetings of their board and archives the meetings on its Web site. The recordings are good quality and a good model for other districts. Share the Web site with your school board and discover a whole new way to keep the community engaged and involved in the business of education.

Details

Audience	School and community
Type	audio
Resource type	informational
Frequency	varies
Source/Author	Minneapolis Public Schools
Location	Minneapolis, MN
Source URL	www.mpls.k12.mn.us/mpsboard.html

School Library Journal

www.schoollibraryjournal.com/article/ca6363460.html

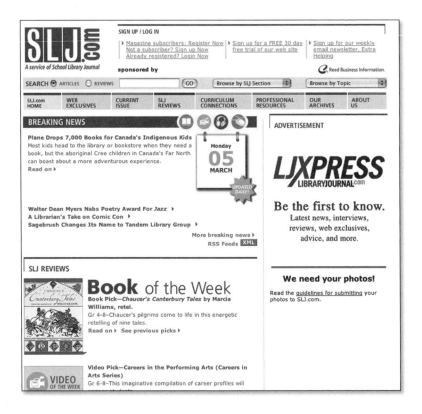

Description

The School Library Journal's podcast series features a variety of inter-views, commentary, reviews, and readings from children's literature. As with most of the site's other content, these podcasts are profession-ally produced and contain well-written content. There's even a series on *School Library 2.0* that features podcast information for librarians. Between podcasts and a full Web site, there is lots to explore here.

Sample Topics

> LibraryThing

> Open Content, Open Conference

> Games in Education

> Library 2.0

Classroom Applications

If you want intelligent conversation about cutting-edge technology, the School Library Journal's podcasts are perfect for you. While the content is focused toward school librarians, anyone in education will benefit from listening to the reviews and readings. The readings, such as J. Patrick Lewis' readings from his *Black Cat Bone: The Life of Blues Legend Robert Johnson*, are wonderful and inspiring for anyone interested in using podcasts for the presentation of literary materials.

Details

Audience	K–12 educators, higher education educators, preservice teachers, media specialists/librarians
Type	audio
Resource type	instructional
Frequency	monthly
Source/Author	School Library Journal
Source URL	www.schoollibraryjournal.com

CHAPTER 5

Podcasts about Educational Technology

Information for technology coordinators, school IT managers and anyone curious about new and emerging technologies

It's surprising that there aren't more podcasts focused on educational technology. What is not so surprising, though, is that the early leaders in the field embraced the technology and many have been podcasting for several years.

In this chapter you'll find podcasts from educators, technology coordinators and educational technology vendors who have unique perspectives on the use and support of podcast technology in schools and districts.

Techintegration.net

http://teachers.ocps.net/lienj/podcasting/podcasting.htm

Description

Professional development centers around the country are jumping on the podcasting bandwagon. Through Techintegration.net, Orange County Public Schools in Florida offers podcasts designed especially for technology coordinators or curriculum. OCPS's *Alpha Geek* series presents tech talk for digital immigrants and offers very nicely presented step-by-step coaching on topics from information literacy to integrating digital literacy.

Sample Topics

> Tech Tools in Education

> WebBlender Help

> The Alpha Geek

Classroom Applications

This site is a great illustration of how professional development can be extended beyond traditional in-classroom content delivery. While there are just a few topics, the podcasts presented on the site are very useful to anyone engaged in introducing podcasting and other technology into classrooms, schools or districts.

Details

Audience	K–12 educators and technology coordinators
Type	audio blog
Resource type	news and events
Frequency	varies, a series
Source/Author	Orange County Public Schools, John Lien
Location	Orlando, FL
Source URL	http://techintegration.net

Conference Connections

Link to podcast through iTunes:
http://phobos.apple.com/WebObjects/MZStore.woa/wa/
viewPodcast?id=213440691

Description

Stay in touch with emerging trends and technologies and discover the most exciting workshops, forums and discussions at leading technology conferences. This podcast series, produced by Apple Distinguished Educators, offers some of the most innovative content from conferences across the USA and around the world. The series begins with the 2007 Florida Educational Technology Conference (FETC) from Orlando, Florida. Additional conference-related materials and resources on the Apple Learning Interchange are available at http://edcommunity.apple.com/ali/.

Sample Presenters

> Dan Schmidt

> David Warlick

Classroom Applications

Experienced educators share profiles of true innovation and success in the classroom. Educators discuss various topics including their use of blogging to inspire their students, an iPod project with ESL students, or how get staff up to speed on professional multimedia applications. These practical examples are from real teachers who are incorporating technology in the classroom to engage and motivate their students.

Details

Audience	K–12 educators and higher education educators
Type	audio
Resource type	instruction
Frequency	varies
Source/Author	Apple Distinguished Educators
Source URL	http://edcommunity.apple.com/ali/

Harvard Extension School: Computer Science Course

www.fas.harvard.edu/~cscie1/

Lectures

Lecture 1: Hardware. Computation. Overview. Bits and bytes. ASCII. Processors. Motherboards: buses, connectors, ports, slots, and sockets. Memory: ROM, RAM, and cache. Available in Flash, MP3 and QuickTime formats, along with jargon and slides in PDF.

Lecture 2: Hardware, Continued. Secondary storage: floppy disks, hard disks (PATA and SATA), CDs, and DVDs. Virtual Memory. Expansion buses and cards: AGP, ISA, PCI, PCI Express, and SCSI. I/O devices. Peripherals. How to shop for a computer. History. Available in Flash, MP3 and QuickTime formats, along with slides in PDF.

Lecture 3: Software. It's the first of two movie nights for Computer Science E-1! A look at "how modern day visionaries Bill Gates and Steve Jobs changed the world" by way of *Pirates of Silicon Valley*, a dramatization of the history of Microsoft Corporation and Apple Computer, Inc. Not available.

Lecture 4: The Internet. Networks: clients and servers, peer-to-peer, LANs and WLANs, the Internet, and domains. Email: addresses; IMAP, POP and SMTP; netiquette; spam; emoticons; snail mail; and listservs. SSH. The World Wide Web: URLs and HTTP. Blogs. Instant messaging. SFTP. Usenet. Available in Flash, MP3 and QuickTime formats, along with jargon and slides in PDF.

Lecture 5: The Internet, Continued. Network topologies. The Internet: backbones, TCP/IP, DHCP, and DNS. NAT. Ethernet: NICs, cabling, switches, routers, and access points. Wireless: IR, RF, Bluetooth, and WiFi. ISPs. Modems: dialup, cable, and DSL. Available in Flash, MP3 and QuickTime formats, along with jargon and slides in PDF.

Lecture 6: Jeopardy! Students versus teaching fellows! Available in Flash, MP3 and QuickTime formats.

Lecture 7: Multimedia. Graphics: file formats, bitmaps and vectors, and compression. Audio: file formats and compression. Video (and audio): file formats and compression. Streaming. Available in Flash, MP3 and QuickTime formats, along with jargon and slides in PDF.

Lecture 8: Security. Threats to privacy: cookies, forms, logs, and data recovery. Security risks: packet sniffing, passwords, phishing, hacking, viruses and worms, spyware, and zombies. Piracy: WaReZ and cracking. Available in Flash, MP3 and QuickTime formats, along with jargon and slides in PDF.

Lecture 9: Security, Continued. Defenses: scrubbing, firewalls, proxy servers, VPNs, cryptography, virus scanners, product registration and activation. Available in Flash, MP3 and QuickTime formats, along with jargon and slides in PDF.

Lecture 10: Website Development. Webservers: structure, permissions, and implementations. Static webpages: XHTML, well-formedness, and validity. Dynamic webpages: SSIs, DHTML, AJAX, CGI, ASPs, and JSPs. Available in Flash, MP3 and QuickTime formats, along with jargon and slides in PDF.

Lecture 11: Programming. Pseudocode. Constructs: instructions, variables, conditions, branches, and loops. Languages: interpreted and compiled. Scratch. Available in Flash, MP3 and QuickTime formats, along with jargon and slides in PDF.

Lecture 12: Pictionary! Students versus teaching fellows! Available in Flash, MP3 and QuickTime formats, along with jargon and slides in PDF.

Lecture 13: Dotcoms. It's the second of two movie nights for Computer Science E-1! A look at the rise and fall of the dotcom era by way of *Startup.com*, a documentary that traces the history of goVWorks.com. Not available.

Lecture 14: Exciting Conclusion. Where were you? Where are you? Where can you go? Available in Flash, MP3 and QuickTime formats, along with slides in PDF.

Computer Science E-1:
Understanding Computers and the Internet
Harvard Extension School

The Podcast
RSS
also available to the public via
Google Video, iTunes, iTunes U, YouTube

Filmed in Cambridge, Massachusetts
September 2006 - January 2007

David J. Malan, Instructor
malan@post.harvard.edu

Rei Diaz, Head Teaching Fellow
Dan Armendariz, Teaching Fellow
Eugenia Kim, Teaching Fellow
Chris Thayer, Editor
Chris Mehl, Videographer

This course is all about understanding: understanding what's going on inside your computer when you flip on the switch, why tech support has you constantly rebooting your computer, how everything you do on the Internet can be watched by others, and how your computer can become infected with a worm just by turning it on. In this course we demystify computers and the Internet, along with their jargon, so that students understand not only what they can do with each but also how it all works and why. Students leave this course armed with a new vocabulary and equipped for further exploration of computers and the Internet. Topics include hardware, software, the Internet, multimedia, security, website development, programming, and dotcoms. This course is designed both for those with little, if any, computer experience and for those who use a computer every day.

syllabus

Problem Sets

Problem Set 1: Hardware. Reinforce your understanding of hardware! Available in PDF.

Problem Set 2: Hardware and Software. Reinforce your understanding of hardware and software! Available in PDF.

Videos of the Week
bite-sized segments on topics related to lectures

Vol. 1: Hardware
Changing PC BIOS Settings. Learn how to access and change a PC's BIOS settings! Available in Flash and QuickTime formats.
Dissecting a PC. Learn what the inside of a PC looks like! Available in Flash and QuickTime formats.
Plugging Everything In. Learn how to connect all those cables to your PC! Available in Flash and QuickTime formats.
Upgrading a PC. Learn how to upgrade a PC! Available in Flash and QuickTime formats.
Upgrading RAM. Learn how to upgrade a computer's RAM! Available in Flash and QuickTime formats.

Vol. 2: Software
Browser Wars. Learn about alternatives to Internet Explorer! Available in Flash and QuickTime formats.
Finding and Installing Windows Updates. Learn how to find and install the latest Windows updates for your PC! Available in Flash and QuickTime formats.
Installing Windows XP. Learn how to install Windows XP on a PC! Available in Flash and QuickTime formats.
Macs versus PCs. Learn about differences between Macs and PCs in this face-off! Available in Flash and QuickTime formats.

Vol. 3: The Internet
Hosting Options. Learn how to select a host for your website! Available in Flash and QuickTime formats.
Registering a Domain Name. Learn how to register a domain name of your own! Available in Flash and QuickTime formats.
Shopping Online. Learn how to shop ('til you drop) online! Available in Flash and QuickTime formats.
Treasure Hunting. Learn how to search the Web more effectively! Available in Flash and QuickTime formats.

Vol. 4: The Internet
HTTP. Learn what http:// is all about! Available in Flash and QuickTime formats.
TCP/IP. Learn how TCP/IP works! Available in Flash and QuickTime formats.
Web Servers. Web Servers! Available in Flash and QuickTime formats.

Vol. 5: Personal Tech
"Alien" Technology. Learn about designing and building a machine from the ground up in this interview with Alienware! Available in Flash and QuickTime formats.
Digital Entertainment. Learn how to digitally entertain! Available in Flash and QuickTime formats.
Home Networking: Part I. Learn how to network your home! Available in Flash and QuickTime formats.
Home Networking: Part II. Learn how to network your home (continued)! Available in Flash and QuickTime formats.

Vol. 6: Multimedia
Buying a Digital Camera. Learn how to shop for a digital camera! Available in Flash and QuickTime formats.
Digital Photography. Learn about digital photography! Available in Flash and QuickTime formats.

Description

Computer Science E-1: *Understanding Computers and the Internet* is a course offered at Harvard University's Extension School. Its course content, available free of charge, covers the basics of technology (specifically computer technology) and guides novice users through the ins and outs of the Internet. The accompanying Web site offers other similar course content too.

Sample Topics

> Virus Protection

> Upgrading RAM

> Browser Wars

> Upgrading a PC

Classroom Applications

Harvard Extension has long been a leader in presenting content in new ways. Its Distance Education Program has provided current information to preservice educators and other students for several years. If you're looking for a way to offer your course content online, this is a good model. Harvard archives all the lectures through iTunes and most lectures feature downloadable content, a podcast on the jargon used, and supporting slides.

Details

Audience	K–12 educators and technology coordinators
Type	video
Resource type	instruction
Frequency	varies
Source/Author	Harvard University Extension School
Location	Cambridge, MA
Source URL	www.fas.harvard.edu/~cscie1/

Podcast for Teachers, Techpod

www.podcastforteachers.org/PFTlisten.html

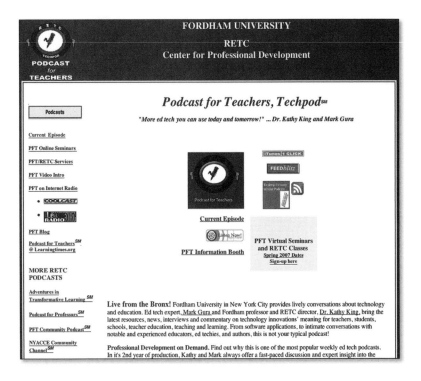

Description

In its *Live, from the Bronx!* podcast Fordham University's Regional Educational Technology Center (RETC) offers interviews and lectures about technology through the voice of leading educators. Podcasts cover how-to content on software applications, interviews with notable or exemplary educators, education technology leaders, and more.

Sample Topics

> Adventures in Transformative Learning

> Control-Shift: From Content Consumer to Producer— Gaming, iPods and Kid Pix, Multitasking

> Tech Gone Wild! Digital Delivery, Digital Media, Digital Controversy.

Classroom Applications

This podcast, presented by a center for professional development, offers so much information about so many things it's almost overwhelming. I enjoyed updates on assistive technology, news about open-source technology, and an update from the RETC's tech personnel on how they're doing with tech implementation. I chose this podcast because it's a very effective model for information dissemination by a regional center and is stuffed with information useful to almost anyone who is involved with technology in K–12 and higher ed.

Details

Audience	K–12, higher education educators and technology coordinators
Type	audio
Resource type	professional
Frequency	monthly
Source/Author	Mark Gura, Kathy King
Location	Fordham University Regional Educational Technology Center, NY
Source URL	www.podcastforteachers.org

Engadget

www.engadget.com/category/podcasts/

Description

This podcast is a collection of technology news from around the world—mostly centering on the latest technologies and breaking news. It's presented monthly in a "digest" format—bite-sized stories collected into one podcast.

Sample Topics

> DirectTV to Unveil SAT-GO

> Palm Treo

> Bluetooth Watches

> Microsoft Zune

Classroom Applications

I spend a huge amount of time, it seems, looking for information. Finding this podcast was a blessing. The information is credible and well presented. Listening to this podcast is a good way to keep up with trends and issues in technology that could impact what does what in your school. While it's decidedly consumer-focused, I usually find out some interesting tidbits to dazzle my technology coordinator friends with.

Details

Audience	K–12 educators and technology coordinators
Type	audio
Resource type	news and events
Frequency	monthly
Source/Author	Engadget staff (Trent Wolbe, Peter Rojas, Ryan Block)
Source URL	www.engadget.com

Soft Reset

www.learninginhand.com/softreset/

Description

This podcast is for any educator who uses a Palm or Windows Mobile handheld computer. Mike Curtis and Tony Vincent offer expert tips and techniques for technology integration and light-hearted discussion about the pitfalls and rewards of using handhelds in classrooms K–12.

Sample Topics

> Mobile Internet

> Pod People (notes from workshops about handhelds and podcasting)

> News from NECC

> Science

Classroom Applications

This podcast is presented by two of my technology idols—Mike Curtis and Tony Vincent. Mike and Tony are incredibly in tune with today's classroom technology—especially handheld computers and can explain just about any concept to anyone in about 30 seconds. If your school uses handhelds or smartphones in education, or is considering the purchase of mobile devices of any kind, this podcast is a "must listen."

Details

Audience	K–12 educators and technology coordinators
Type	audio
Resource type	teaching tools
Frequency	about once a week
Source/Author	Tony Vincent, Mike Curtis
Source URL	www.learninginhand.com

Cut to the Core: Essential Podcasts for Educators

Link to podcast through iTunes:
**http://phobos.apple.com/WebObjects/MZStore.woa/wa/
viewPodcast?id=154586042**

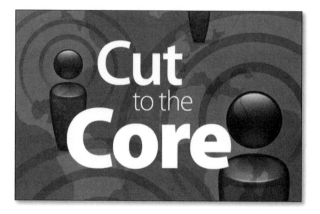

Description

Cut to the Core is brought to you by Apple Distinguished Educators from around the world. This podcast showcases current trends, innovative strategies, and replicable ideas that will empower educators to transform classrooms of the 21st century.

Sample Presenters

> Dr. Alan Brightman

> Dr. Milton Chen

> Mark Prensky

Classroom Applications

Sometimes hearing information and practical examples of using technology in the classroom from your peers is the best way to hit the ground running. This podcast is appropriate for professional development support, for keeping up to speed on the latest technologies for education, and to hear from "experts" about how podcasting, blogging, multimedia and other applications are engaging and motivating students (and teachers) everywhere.

Details

Audience	K–12 educators and higher education educators
Type	audio
Resource type	information/instruction
Frequency	varies
Source/Author	Apple Distinguished Educators
Location	varies
Source URL	http://edcommunity.apple.com/ali/

Teach with Tech

www.indiana.edu/~icy/podcast/

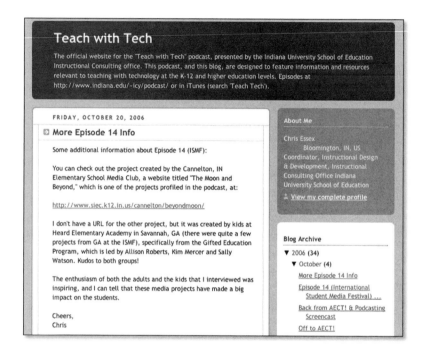

Description

Indiana University School of Education's Instructional Consulting Office presents a podcast designed to help education faculty, preservice and inservice educators integrate all kinds of technology into teaching and learning. Podcasts contain a wide variety of useful information including featured Web site reviews and discussions of emerging technologies. The accompanying Web site (a blog) offers links to all the items mentioned in each podcast.

Sample Topics

> Teaching with Wikis, Running with Leopard

> Tips for Using Technology in Your Classroom Tomorrow

> College Teaching Tech Tips

Classroom Applications

One of the best things about this podcast is the supporting information on the Web site. The presenter is meticulous about offering links to every site or technology mentioned in each broadcast and the episodes are brief but packed with information. The presenter, Chris Essex, is the very well-informed Coordinator of Instructional Design & Development in the university's Instructional Consulting Office, at the Indiana University School of Education.

Details

Audience	K–12, higher education educators, technology coordinators
Type	audio
Resource type	instructional, blog
Frequency	about once a week
Source/Author	Christopher Essex, Indiana University School of Education
Source URL	www.teachwtech.blogspot.com

ISTE Webinar Podcasts

www.iste.org/Content/NavigationMenu/Membership/
Webinar_Series/ISTE_Webinars.htm

Description

Join ISTE for a series of "meet the author" chats featuring ISTE authors and other guests.

Sample Topics

> Handheld Computers and Smartphones in Secondary Schools: A Guide to Hands-on Learning

> Strategies for Building a Successful 1-to-1 Computing Program

> Teaching with Digital Images: Acquire, Analyze, Create, Communicate

Classroom Applications

It's one thing to read a book, another to actually hear the author and get to ask questions. ISTE offers the opportunity to attend live events, via webinars (later archived), with leading authors of books published through ISTE. Topics range from handheld computers to open-source operating systems in education.

Details

Audience	K–12 educators and technology coordinators
Type	audio blog
Resource type	news and events
Frequency	varies—a series
Source/Author	ISTE and special guests
Location	Eugene, OR
Source URL	www.iste.org

Edupodder

feed://www.edupodder.com/edupodder_rss.xml

Description

From the hallways and pizza joints around San Jose State University, this podcast offers a look at key issues in podcasting and notes from students taking courses in journalism and communications at SJSU. The topics vary greatly from technology discussions to conversations with key school personnel related to podcasting and other technologies.

Sample Topics

> Emerging Technology: A Podcast while doing a Podcast

> RSS

> Perspectives of an Indian Student at SJSU

> New Media Journalism Class (Pizzacast 2.0)

> Linux on Campus

Classroom Applications

This is a podcast for the hard-core techies out there or for anyone who might enjoy a college student perspective on emerging technologies. Mostly unedited but nicely produced segments offer insight into a key Silicon Valley university's use of technology for instruction, administration and learning.

Details

Audience	higher education faculty, students, administration; K–12 technology coordinators
Type	audio
Resource type	instructional
Frequency	monthly
Source/Author	Steve Sloan
Location	San Jose, CA
Source URL	www.edupodder.com

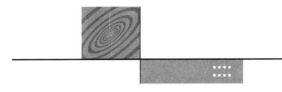

CHAPTER 6

Podcasts for Mathematics

Lots of numbers, symbols,
and formulas in your ear

You might not think that podcasting and math are a good match. Au contraire! The Internet offers access to podcasts covering topics such as using math in everyday life and tutorials about specifics in geometry, calculus and more. These podcasts are useful for early learners all the way to higher education.

Mathtutor

www.mathtutor.ac.uk/ipod.shtml

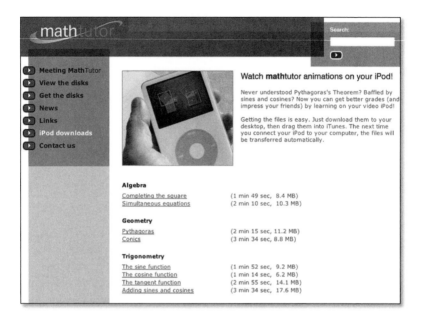

Description

Key math concepts—one minute at a time. This site offers basic tutorial help in algebra, geometry, trigonometry and calculus. The presentation is clear and the math flawless with video examples of each concept.

Sample Topics

> Completing the Square

> Pythagoras

> The Cosine Function

> The Gradient of a Curve

> Estimating Areas

Classroom Applications

Sometimes a second run through complex content helps. This site offers short segments of instruction, delivered by a quite articulate Englishman, with video and audio examples. Be sure to coach your students to expect those wonderful differences in language—you'll hear anti-clockwise (counterclockwise) and theta (thay-tuh) pronounced thee-tuh, for example. I found students actually paid MORE attention because of these elements.

Details

Audience	6–12 and higher education
Type	video
Resource type	instructional
Frequency	special
Source/Author	Shaun Canon
Location	London, England
Source URL	www.mathtutor.ac.uk

College Mathematics (MAT 142)

http://tiger.la.asu.edu/podcast/

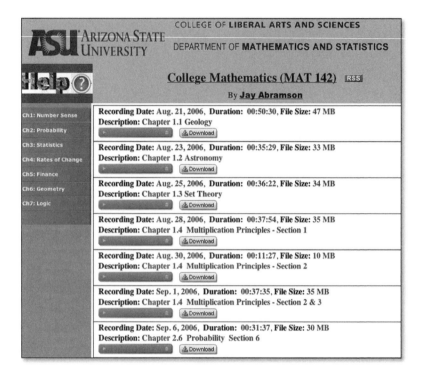

Description

Arizona State University offers podcasts of college lectures in several curriculum areas. This series features math concepts for students who need basic discussion of principles and lots of examples. The lectures are well structured and the professor uses real-world examples to make the learning more relevant and fun. A graphing calculator at the ready is an essential tool for accompanying the lectures.

Sample Topics

> Astronomy and Math

> Multiplication Principles

> Set Theory

Classroom Applications

I like these lectures because the professor's presentation is light and concise. These lectures would be very good for advanced Grade 9–12 students as a review of topics from multiplication principles to probability. If your school or university is looking for a model, this might be a good one. The professor begins each lesson by informing the students that "the tape recorder is on" and then pauses a moment to get ready—then launches into the lesson. You might consider listening to a few and creating a quiz to check understanding after each lesson.

Details

Audience	higher education or advanced secondary students
Type	audio
Resource type	instructional
Frequency	daily
Source/Author	Arizona State University, Dept. of Mathematics, Jay Abramson
Source URL	http://tiger.la.asu.edu/podcast/

Dan's Mathcast

www.dansmath.com/pages/podpage.html

dansmath > pages > **podcast page**

dansmath
.com

d ͡a n s
m A th
c A s t

mathematics
for the
masses

"dansmathcast" >< *dan's math podcast* >< *on the air since nov 2005*

| what in the world is a podcast? | how can I listen to dansmathcast? | what's so special about dansmathcast? | just what goes into a dansmathcast? | show notes and blog for dansmathcast | cast vote on podcast alley for dansmathcast |

What is a podcast?

Podcasting is a new form of communication; basically it's like a radio **show** on your TiVo. Podcasters can **record**, film, and/or save their creative efforts, and users can then **subscribe** or **download**, and listen at their convenience.

You don't need an iPod to listen to podcasts! There are also 'enhanced' and video podcasts! download my show promo here (500KB)

Description

Presented by Dan Bach, a community college math teacher at Diablo Valley College in Pleasant Hill, California, this podcast is a collection of news, events, and challenge problems based on real-world math. Examples are delivered, then explained, and challenge problems offer opportunities for moving into more advanced math. While most podcasts are audio-only, Dan offers a couple of video segments as well.

Sample Topics

> Astronomy and Math

> Multiplication Principles

> Logarithms

Classroom Applications

Dan's conversational tone and real-world examples make this an excellent site for review of basic math concepts for high school or college students. The pace is rapid, so try this one out on your more advanced students or those that need review. Of course, it's a digital podcast, so students can listen over and over again. Have a graphing calculator handy while you listen and you can work along with Dan.

Details

Audience	K–12 and higher education students
Type	audio/video
Resource type	instructional
Frequency	2 times per month
Source/Author	Dan Bach
Location	Pleasant Hill, CA
Source URL	www.dansmath.com

Mathgrad.com

Link to podcast through iTunes:
http://phobos.apple.com/WebObjects/MZStore.woa/wa/
viewPodcast?id=117406061&s=143441

Description

Christopher Frederick, a graduate student from Colorado State University, presents a math podcast focusing on short lessons on basic math principles. There's an introductory segment, a math concept segment, and, often, a problem of the week.

Sample Topics

> › Sudoku

> › Zeno's Paradox

> › The Poincare Conjecture

> › The Mathematics of Maps

> › Size, Scale, and 100-Foot Insects

> › Intro to Probability

Classroom Applications

This podcast is a fresh look at everyday math problems. Chris covers topics in basic math, like probability and surface area, and problems sent in by listeners. His segments on Sudoku and factorials are particularly good introductions. His pacing is slow and excellent for most Grade 7–12 or higher education students. Be sure to have a pencil, paper and calculator on hand when you or your students listen.

Details

Audience	K–12 and higher education students
Type	audio
Resource type	instructional
Frequency	about two times per month
Source/Author	Christopher Frederick
Location	Colorado State University, Fort Collins, CO
Source URL	www.mathgrad.com

The Math Factor

http://mathfactor.uark.edu

Description

This podcast is actually a real, live radio broadcast that airs on KUAF 91.3 FM from Fayetteville, Arkansas. The program offers a "puzzle approach" to basic math presented by a math professor at the University of Arkansas. Each puzzle is presented, then the answer, including how to work things out, is offered along the way, or in the following week's podcast.

Sample Topics

> Catching Errors

> The Shape of the Universe

> The Most Powerful Force

> Trap Door Encryption

Classroom Applications

This podcast cleverly disguises the dreaded "word problem" as a puzzle for listeners. Puzzles are a great way to offer application of basic math skills in an environment that's non-threatening and, perhaps, competitive. High school and college students could work in groups or as individuals to solve the weekly problems presented. The quality of this broadcast is very high (sound, pacing, production) and is a great example of quality to strive for.

Details

Audience	6–12 and higher education students
Type	audio
Resource type	instructional
Frequency	weekly
Source/Author	C. Goodman-Strauss and Kyle Kellams
Location	Fayetteville, AR
Source URL	http://mathfactor.uark.edu

CHAPTER 7

Podcasts for Science

Everything from NASA to microbes, in pod-sized chunks

Whether you're a science teacher or looking for interdisciplinary activities to incorporate across the curriculum, science podcasts are a great way to strengthen your activities. There are many more podcasts available for science teachers than most of the other curriculum areas in both audio and video formats. You'll find everything from the usual suspects like NASA and *Scientific American* to the classroom teacher who's sharing tips and techniques.

Astronomy a Go-Go!

http://astronomy.libsyn.com

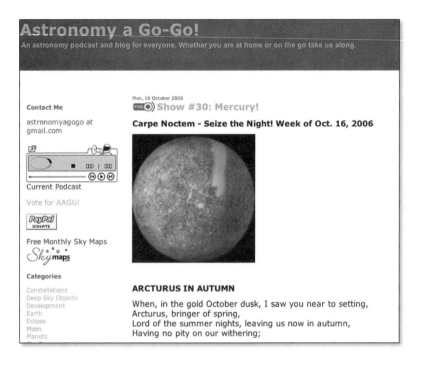

Description

This podcast covers key concepts in astronomy, as well as news, events and viewing activities keyed to the current date. During each show, host Alice Few presents new music and activities to go along with information and viewing tips. The show notes include sky map links and a list of objects and music presented.

Sample Topics

> Distance to the Planets by Halves

> Tour of the Sky (for the current month)

> Classroom Applications

The accompanying Web site offers a HUGE amount of information and background for each show including everything from poetry to star charts to graphs. The shows labeled *Tour of the Sky* offer coordinates and coaching for novice telescope users and excellent science background describing what you're viewing. The way the podcast is presented is perfect for hobbyists and astronomy students alike. The content is perfect for parent/student activities at home.

Details

Audience	K–12 and higher education students, parents
Type	audio
Resource type	instructional
Frequency	varies
Source/Author	Alice Few
Source URL	http://astronomy.libsyn.com

The Jodcast

www.jodcast.net

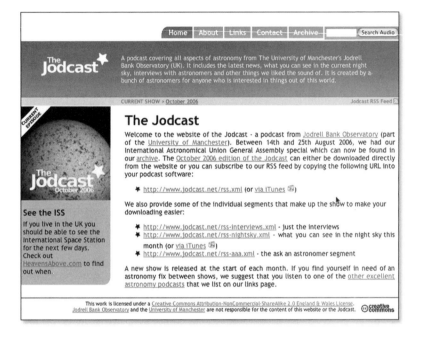

Description

Astronomy from the source. Join astronomers from the University of Manchester's Jodrell Bank Observatory (UK) for news updates, interviews with prominent astronomers, and lively discussions of anything out of this world. The podcast features night-sky viewing tips, listener questions, and much more.

Sample Topics

> › Control Room Tour

> › The Night Sky for September

Classroom Applications

I like this podcast because it covers a wide range of astronomy topics each week. It's also available in six languages, including French, Hindi, and Portuguese. The British accents somehow make even the more complex issues seem fathomable for students and teachers. This show is a perfect resource for amateur and professional astronomy buffs, and students studying basic astronomy. The Jodrell Observatory Web site also hosts a wide range of images and maps to help you better understand the broadcasts.

Details

Audience	K–12 and higher education students
Type	audio
Resource type	instructional
Frequency	monthly
Source/Author	Jodrell Bank Observatory
Location	University of Manchester, Manchester, England
Source URL	www.jodcast.net

The Wild Classroom

www.thewildclassroom.com/home/nav/podastingscience.html

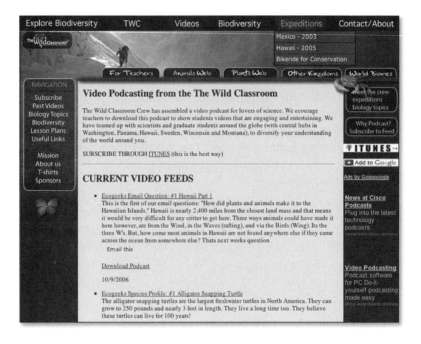

Description

A crew of science teachers explores science topics with audio and video podcasts direct on-location in exotic places such as Panama, Hawaii, Sweden, and the less exotic, but just as interesting Wisconsin and Montana. The accompanying Web site hosts lesson plans and lots of great links to other related resources.

Sample Topics

> EcoGeeks: Alligator Snapping Turtle

> EcoGeeks: Hawaii

> EcoGeeks: Streams and Rivers

Classroom Applications

The programs feature very enthusiastic science educators presenting science facts and doing interviews, making observations, and DOING science in some pretty impressive locations. The production is amazing—on par with some of the National Geographic tours—but produced with a small budget by the two university science wizards. A sister site, called *Explore Biodiversity* (www.explorebiodiversity.com) also offers content focusing specifically on the diversity of plant and animal life in the locations they visit.

Details

Audience	K–12 students
Type	video
Resource type	instructional
Frequency	monthly
Source/Author	Hazen Audel and Rob Nelson
Location	Spokane, WA
Source URL	www.thewildclassroom.com

AccessMedicine

http://books.mcgraw-hill.com/podcast/acm/

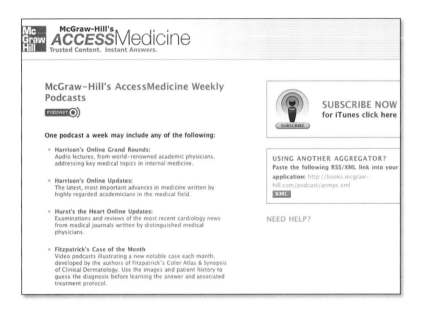

Description

This Web site is designed as a resource for medical students, residents, clinicians, and researchers and provides training, updates, interviews, lectures, and Q&A from trusted sources around the world. The video podcasts feature a wide range of topics including surgery updates, research in medicine, key medical topics, and updates on what's happening in pharmacology and with clinical trials.

Sample Topics

> Online Metabolic and Molecular Bases of Inherited Disease

> Nonalcoholic Fatty Liver Disease

> The Usefulness of Various ECG Leads for Measuring QT Prolongation

Classroom Applications

This podcast is a prime example of a podcast that provides learning access to inservice professionals and the growing trend of offering supplemental content alongside standard textbooks. While the level of this content is decidedly for higher education and beyond, Grade 9–12 students might benefit from snippets from podcasts as they find out more about how hospitals and medicine really work. The online update segment each week provides a look at the latest advances in medicine and health and might be useful to health teachers at any level.

Details

Audience	K–12 health teachers, higher education—medical students,
Type	video
Resource type	instructional
Frequency	weekly
Source/Author	McGraw-Hill Publishers
Source URL	www.mhprofessional.com

Science Update Podcast

www.scienceupdate.com/podcast.php

Description

The AAAS Science Update Podcast features five stories about the latest discoveries in science, technology and medicine. The podcast, based on a popular radio show heard daily on stations around the U.S., is written for anyone who appreciates science and wants to know more about the world around them.

Sample Topics

> › Monster Truck

> › Aliens

> › Doctor's Office

Classroom Applications

This short show is guaranteed to pique the interest of just about anyone. A recent podcast talked about such diverse topics as highly trained bees and bomb detection and the chemicals in a Stradivarius violin. Students in Grades K–12 might use the podcast for everything from science trivia to science fair project ideas.

Details

Audience	K–12 students
Type	audio
Resource type	instructional
Frequency	monthly
Source/Author	American Association for the Advancement of Science
Source URL	www.scienceupdate.com

Science on the Wild Side Podcast

http://scienceonthewildsideshow.libsyn.com

Description

Each podcast features news, science stories, and humorous educational songs from the Singing Science Teacher. Designed primarily for elementary and middle school students, the short segments might be a great way to enhance the study of one of the many topics covered on the site.

Sample Topics

> Virus Bug Blues

> Salute to Caves & Cave Critters

> Salute to Anacondas

Classroom Applications

This site is truly unique, not only because it's one of the few to cater to Grade K–8 learning and science, but also because it's, well, musical. The seventh-grade science educator, Rick Quarles, offers a tune with each podcast to educate and entertain the audience. You'll get both a giggle and lots of good information from this creative use of podcast technology.

Details

Audience	K–8 students
Type	audio
Resource type	instructional
Frequency	biweekly
Source/Author	Rick Quarles
Source URL	http://scienceonthewildside.com

EMS People do Cool Stuff!

www.ems.psu.edu/features/podcast-video.xml

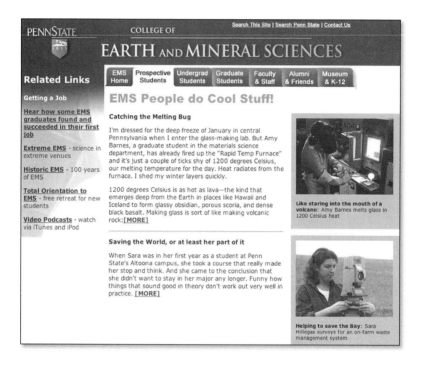

Description

Penn State's College of Earth and Mineral Sciences (EMS) offers a video perspective on how scientists, engineers and other professionals work together in a program designed to help students study the environment. The podcast topics often feature students sharing their excitement about choosing science careers and areas of study.

Sample Topics

> EMS Extreme Science

> Digging in the Lake-bottom Mud

Classroom Applications

While the podcast is primarily designed for internal collegiate audiences (with lots of interesting and colorful references to the campus), it's a very good example of what student might expect when they begin the study of science in higher education institutions. One particular segment features a first-year meteorology student going behind the scenes as a weatherman at the Campus Weather Service. This podcast is a great way to introduce career education into the curriculum.

Details

Audience	K–12 and higher education students
Type	video
Resource type	instructional
Frequency	biweekly
Source/Author	Penn State University
Location	University Park, PA
Source URL	www.ems.psu.edu

Scientific American: 60-Second Science

www.sciam.com/podcast/

Description

One of the leading science magazines presents short segments about the latest developments in science and technology. The one-minute segments cover short subjects in space and physics, health, biology, archaeology, and more.

Sample Topics

> Nobel Laureates

> Ancient Nanotechnology

> Einstein's Right on Time

> Evolution Quiets Crickets

> Pirate Science

Classroom Applications

At only a minute long, this podcast focuses on a single story or concept and gives just enough information to tickle the imagination. These segments are perfect for beginning discussion, or kick-starting research on topics relevant to your curriculum. The segments are well produced, well written and a nice model for a bite-sized broadcast. This is also a great podcast to listen to on your way to class—it'll give you good ideas and things to talk about.

Details

Audience	K–12, higher education students, educators, general public
Type	audio
Resource type	news and events
Frequency	daily
Source/Author	Scientific American editors
Location	varies
Source URL	www.sciam.com

NASAcast

www.nasa.gov/multimedia/podcasting/

Description

Stay connected to what's new at the National Aeronautics and Space Administration. This podcast offers a wide variety of minute-long updates on research, shuttle flights, the space station, space research and much more.

Sample Topics

> Video of Shuttle Flights

> This Week at NASA

> Space Trivia

Classroom Applications

NASA has long been the mother lode of information about all things space. Now it has embraced podcasting technology to do something wonderful with an update podcast. If you or your students are tracking shuttle flights, monitoring launches, or are curious about the many research and development efforts at NASA, this well-organized and well-presented podcast is for you. NASA's Web site offers a wealth of other audio and video content too.

Details

Audience	K–12, higher education students, educators, general public
Type	audio/video
Resource type	instructional
Frequency	varies
Source/Author	NASA
Source URL	www.nasa.gov

Instant Anatomy

www.instantanatomy.net/podcasts.html

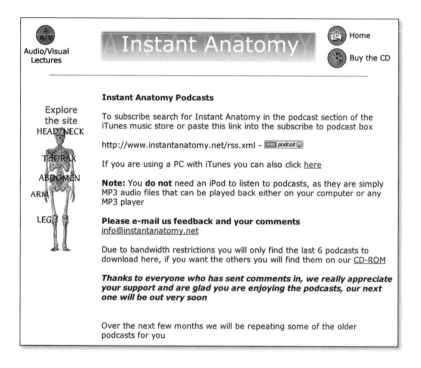

Description

Cambridge University presents continuing education courses in human anatomy. The course material is very high level and can accompany simple or complex lab or dissection work.

Sample Topics

> Nerve Damage in Humeral Fractures

> The Knee Joint

> Small Muscles of the Hand

> Vertebral Column

Curriculum Applications

Podcasts are increasingly part of continuing educator for professionals like doctors, lawyers and educators. This site focuses on high-level content in human anatomy and, while designed primarily for continuing education for physicians, could be terrific for use in advanced-level Grade K–12 biology or higher-ed anatomy or physiology courses. It might also be useful for an identification exercise where students take note of medical/physiological terms and sketch or define.

Details

Audience	K–12, higher education students, educators, general public
Type	video
Resource type	instructional
Frequency	archived
Source/Author	Cambridge University
Location	Cambridge, England
Source URL	www.instantanatomy.net

Brain Food Podcast

www.brainfoodpodcast.com

Description

This podcast is a collection of science facts and commonly asked questions in mathematics, chemistry, physics, and other sciences. The material is presented in a newscast-like fashion and the segments, while short, are packed full of material.

Sample Topics

> Anatomy of the Eye

> Sunsets

> Clocks

> Particle Accelerators

Curriculum Applications

Unlike the college-level podcasts that give you deep-dives into anatomy and physiology, this podcast, designed for a more beginning audience, offers basic science explanations for common questions such as how does the eye work and what is a particle accelerator. Grade K–12 students will enjoy the high-energy theme music and quick pace.

Details

Audience	K–12, higher education students, educators, general public
Type	video
Resource type	instructional
Frequency	weekly
Source/Author	Kyle Butler
Location	Ontario, Canada
Source URL	www.brainfoodpodcast.com

CHAPTER 8

Podcasts for English/ Language Arts

Hear a children's book read by a celebrity, get ideas for writing

Podcasts add a new dimension to teaching and learning in English, composition, grammar, and literature. Books come alive as they are read and activities surrounding those books are enhanced with student- and teacher-created podcast content.

Childrensbookradio.com

www.childrensbookradio.com

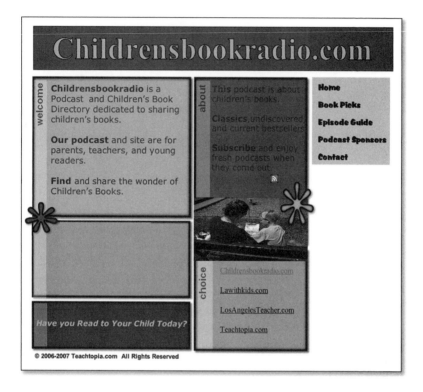

© 2006-2007 Teachtopia.com All Rights Reserved

Description

Childrensbookradio is a podcast dedicated to discussing the world of children's books. Each week, the podcast features a classic and/or current children's book, accompanied by listener reviews and tips on upcoming publications. The Web site has an extensive archive of past episodes.

Sample Topics

> Pippi Longstocking

> The Giving Tree

> Roxaboxen

Classroom Applications

This discussion, hosted by a mother of young twins, offers insights and reviews extremely useful for anyone looking for ideas for children's books in the classroom. It's the parent perspective that makes this podcast really special. The host often gives tips for other Web sites useful for educators as well.

Details

Audience	K–6 students and educators
Type	audio
Resource type	instructional, informational
Frequency	weekly
Source/Author	Children's Book Radio
Source URL	www.childrensbookradio.com

PoetryFoundation.org

http://poetryfoundation.org/features/audio.html

Description

Weekly podcasts from PoetryFoundation.org feature high-quality recordings of poems, interviews, and poetry documentaries. The presentations flow like a fast-paced newscast and also feature tips for other sites across the Web where you'll find information about classic and modern poetry and poets.

Sample Topics

> A Tribute to Czelaw Milosz

> Gabriel Preil

> Remembering Stanley Kunitz

Classroom Applications

As a fan of poetry, I really like the Web site that goes with this podcast. The site, like the podcast, offers access to a wide variety of poetry. The high-quality podcasts offer many examples of poetry, some read by the poet, and a few surprises. One podcast (12/5/06), for example, offered rare recordings of Tennyson, Yeats, Langston-Hughes, and more. Teachers can excerpt, with citation of course, segments for broadcast in the classroom or suggest the site as a research source when studying modern poetry.

Details

Audience	K–12 and higher education educators, 9–12 and higher education students
Type	audio
Resource type	instructional, informational
Frequency	weekly
Source/Author	Poetry Foundation, Curtis Fox
Location	Chicago, IL
Source URL	http://poetryfoundation.org

Shakespeare-upon-iPod

www.shakespearebyanothername.com/audio.html

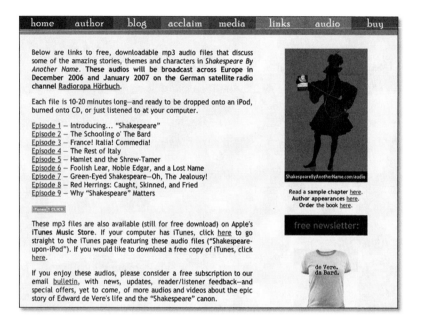

Description

This series, based on the published biography *Shakespeare By Another Name,* introduces nine discussions and readings that focus on the life story of Elizabethan playwright Edward de Vere, Earl of Oxford—the man who many believe wrote under the pen name William Shakespeare.

Sample Topics

> Introducing... Shakespeare

> The Schooling o' The Bard

> France! Italia! Commedia!

> The Rest of Italy

> Hamlet and the Shrew-Tamer

> Foolish Lear, Noble Edgar, and a Lost Name

> Green-Eyed Shakespeare—Oh, The Jealousy!

> Red Herrings: Caught, Skinned, and Fried

> Why Shakespeare Matters

Classroom Applications

This podcast is unique in that it presents a different perspective on William Shakespeare—suggesting that the moniker was a nom de plume for Elizabethan playwright Edward de Vere (Earl of Oxford). The podcasts suggest lots of interesting evidence to back up the claim—things such as the lack of any manuscripts. The site is not a reading of Shakespeare's works, but more a collection of facts to back up the hypothesis about de Vere. It's a compelling puzzle for students and teachers. Was there really a Shakespeare?

Details

Audience	9–12 and higher education students
Type	audio
Resource type	instructional
Frequency	special
Source/Author	Mark Anderson
Source URL	www.shakespearebyanothername.com

Storynory: iPod-Ready Stories for Kids

www.storynory.com/archives

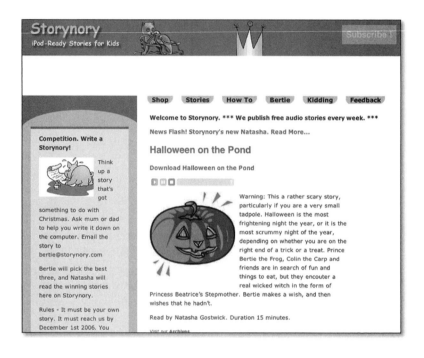

Description

A collection of children's short stories read by lively readers. The site offers free audio stories for kids, ranging from popular classics, such as *The Princess and the Pea*, to lesser-known children's books. The accompanying Web site also offers reviews and more than 100 stories in archive.

Sample Topics

> Alice in Wonderland

> Troy

> Harry and Rosie Take a Train

> Noah's Ark

> Two Poems about Mice

> Hansel and Gretel

> The Gingerbread Man

> Prince Bertie and the Dragon

> The Maiden and the Frog

> The Cat and the Mouse in Partnership

Classroom Applications

You and your students won't be disappointed as you listen to the classic fairy tales and other works read in a lilting British accent complimented by near-perfect diction. The pace is perfect for younger students and the variety of stories available on the site is great. The podcast presents a good model for reading stories for later listening. Students with low vision and anyone else who loves good children's stories will love this site.

Details

Audience	K–12, higher education students, educators, general public
Type	audio
Resource type	instructional
Frequency	varies, a series
Source/Author	NPR staff and guests
Location	varies
Source URL	www.storynory.com

Radio Disney Now!

http://radio.disney.go.com/music/podcast.html

Description

A light-hearted interview series with young celebrities. Promises up-close and personal discussions with the hottest artists, bands, and celebrities, through exclusive interviews. The decidedly Disney-esque style (lots of dazzle, glitz, and glamour) keeps students' attention and offers a few nuggets of wisdom.

Sample Topics

> Aaron Carter Talks About Dirt Bike Racing

> The Olsen Twins Chat About Their Lives as Child Stars

Classroom Applications

OK, so this isn't very intellectual, but students love it. The production quality is also excellent, typical for Disney's high standards. This is a great model for podcast production—a quality and structure to strive for. As for the content, perhaps you might do some analysis on interview and questioning skills?

Details

Audience	K–12, higher education students, educators, general public
Type	audio
Resource type	news and events
Frequency	about once a week
Source/Author	Disney
Source URL	http://radio.disney.go.com

Princeton Review Podcasts

www.princetonreview.com/podcasts/

Description

The pros at the Princeton Review present a variety of podcasts that help students increase their vocabulary, gain insight and practice with the LSAT, or help parents and teachers grab tips for studying for standardized tests.

Sample Topics

> Vocabulary Minute:

- House Party

- Tempo

- The Hectic Day

- Take the "I" Away from Trains

> LSAT in Everyday Life:

- Health Craze

- True Colors

- Cross Words

Classroom Applications

I like the short segments for *Vocabulary Minute*. One example, entitled *Quiet and Loud*, consists of an instructional song—a la *Grammar Rock* but centered on differences in vocabulary surrounding noise such as silence, cacophony, and in between. LSAT segments offer direct examples of how logic operates in real life—a terrific way to show high school students the missing link between what is tested and what occurs in the world around them.

Details

Audience	K–12 students, parents
Type	audio
Resource type	instructional
Frequency	varies
Source/Author	Princeton Review
Source URL	www.princetonreview.com

Reading Rockets

www.readingrockets.org/podcasts/

Description

Reading Rockets offers specific tips and techniques for teaching reading to younger students. Using video clips from Reading Rockets' PBS television series *Launching Young Readers,* the vodcast captures examples of how effective educators use games, simulations, and other fun activities for basic reading skills.

Sample Topics

> Print Awareness

> The Sounds of Speech

> Phonemic Awareness

> Phonics

> Informal Assessment

> Author Interviews with:

- Jack Prelutsky (It's Raining Pigs & Noodles)

- Eve Bunting (Fly Away Home)

- Bruce Degen (Magic School Bus)

Classroom Applications

Carrying the pedigree of super-high quality production and excellent teacher-focused content presented through a grant from the U.S. Department of Education, these podcasts go inside classrooms and offer real-world examples of activities and games. This unique "fly on the wall" scenario allows the viewer to pick up effective techniques and see pitfalls in different lesson formats. The podcasts are particularly useful for preservice educators and any educator working with ESL or special-needs students.

Details

Audience	K–6 educators, preservice educators
Type	audio/video
Resource type	instructional
Frequency	varies
Source/Author	PBS
Source URL	www.readingrockets.org

The Bob and Rob Show

http://englishcaster.com/bobrob/

The Bob and Rob Show
Weekly English Lessons from a Yankee and a Brit.
Bob   Rob

Home | About & Contact | New! Discussion Board |

Ads by Google Phrasal Verbs English Idioms Spoken English Grammar Lesson

Join

Lesson 56: The Bomb.
Oct 19th, 2006 | The Bob and Rob Show | 1 Comment

◄ Listen | Study Guide

Learn how to survive a nuclear attack (really!), the phrasal verb "wipe out", and a protest song.

Song: The Bell , by Stephan Smith

Lesson 55: To Your Health!
Oct 13th, 2006 | The Bob and Rob Show | 6 Comments

◄ Listen | Study Guide

All sorts of stuff about health, including a new drug that lets you appreciate life more. Great song about health, too.

Song: Health to the Company , by the Brobdingnagians

Special thanks to The Wacky Watermelon for the Crap Pharm spoof.

Become a Bob and Rob Show Member!

From Sept. 1st, all podcasts will have an 8-10 page **Study Guide**. Each Guide will have:

* show transcripts
* glossary
* cultural notes
* extra study materials

Learn more!

Members Login

Username:
Password:
Lost password? (Login)

Tags

Description

A tongue-in-cheek podcast by a Yankee and a Brit centering on slang and idioms. The podcast takes the form of a variety show, performed live. Bob and Rob are colorful teachers who live in Japan, where they both teach English at the same university. This is an excellent way to use entertaining content to teach concepts like idioms, slang and word play.

Sample Topics

> Clean Bill of Health

> Sweet Tooth

> Autumn

Classroom Applications

The podcast is funny and it's supported by very good quality teaching materials—two criteria that make this podcast very interesting for educators, especially those who teach ESL or vocabulary studies.

Details

Audience	9–12, ESOL students and educators
Type	audio
Resource type	instructional
Frequency	varies
Source/Author	Bob and Rob (English teachers)
Location	Tokyo, Japan
Source URL	http://englishcaster.com

CHAPTER 9

Podcasts for Social Sciences

*Oral history, deep dives into facts
about the world, geography and more*

Social Studies podcast content is as varied
and broad as the field of study. You'll find
podcasts on geography, history, sociology, and
lots more. There is rich content available from
the gold standards like National Geography and
content for Grade K–12 students provided by
college professors. You'll even find historical
trivia podcasts; and for government, civics, and
law courses, a podcast of the president's weekly
radio message.

iHistory Podcast Project

http://ihistory.wordpress.com/tag/podcasts/

Description

iHistory is a project of Eaglehawk Secondary College in Bendigo, Australia. It offers local history tours presented in podcast format by a very creative high school teacher.

Sample Topics

> Australian Bushrangers

> Old Bendigo Gaol

> Convicts in Australia

Classroom Applications

The blog Web site (http://ihistory.wordpress.com) is a great companion to these unique podcasts focusing on the history of Australia and New Zealand. The Aussie instructor delivers tongue-in-cheek tours with specific background that's a rare glimpse into how history is taught outside the U.S. Students and teachers can use this podcast as a model for local history podcasts, or in their study of World History.

Details

Audience	7–12 students and educators
Type	audio
Resource type	news and events
Frequency	weekly
Source/Author	Eaglehawk SC (secondary school)
Location	Bendigo, Australia
Source URL	http://ihistory.wordpress.com

The Rise and Fall of Jim Crow

www.pbs.org/wnet/jimcrow/stories_narratives.html

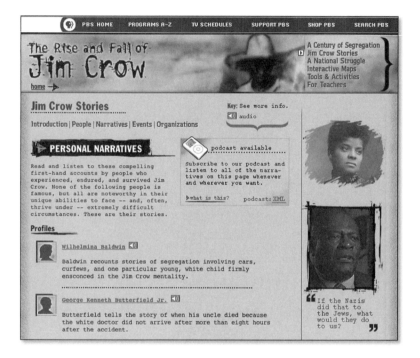

Description

Personal narratives from people who experienced, endured, and survived Jim Crow. Jim Crow wasn't a person, but the personification of a system of government-sanctioned racial oppression and segregation in the U.S. The perspectives presented in these podcasts are real and well supported with maps, tools, lesson plans, and more.

Sample Topics

> Thriving Under Difficult Circumstances

> Personal Narratives

Classroom Applications

A blend of oral history and unique perspectives make these highly compelling podcasts perfect for history classes. The interactive maps and background tools on the site are very useful in the classroom. Some of the interviews are thought provoking, others disturbing. Be sure to listen these prior to assigning them to your class. They're quite powerful.

Details

Audience	K–12 and higher education students
Type	audio
Resource type	curriculum
Frequency	one-time
Source/Author	PBS
Source URL	www.pbs.org/wnet/jimcrow/

Military History Podcast

www.militaryhistorypodcast.blogspot.com

Description

A collection of podcasts about current and historical events presented by an unlikely and very professional correspondent—a teenager. Each segment is short and covers a single topic.

Sample Topics

> Iraq Study Group

> U.S. Secret Service

> Propaganda

> Raptors and Spirits

Classroom Applications

The most amazing thing about this podcast is that it's scripted and presented by a 15-year-old student. George Hageman offers content in a steady, serious tone and is extremely well organized and articulate. This podcast is excellent for use in history classes studying war and conflict and for introducing high school students to historical trends and issues.

Details

Audience	K–12 and higher education students
Type	audio
Resource type	curriculum
Frequency	one-time
Source/Author	George Hageman
Location	Arlington, VA
Source URL	www.militaryhistorypodcast.blogspot.com

Talking History

feed://talkinghistory.oah.org/podcast-2006.xml

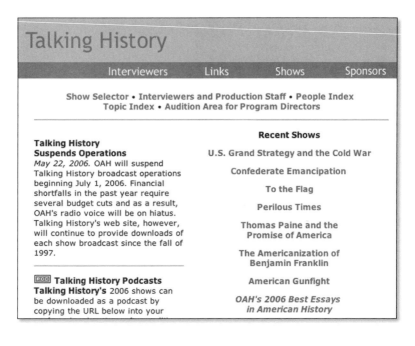

Description

A podcast presented through the auspices of the University of Missouri and the radio voice of the OAH Organization of American Historians. The host offers insight, interviews and perspective on social change, war, and other historical elements that impact the fabric of American life.

Sample Topics

> Thomas Paine and the Promise of America

> Confederate Emancipation

> To the Flag

Classroom Applications

While there are quite a few podcasts that present perspectives on history, this one's a favorite because the segments are so well written and you'll leave each one with interesting tidbits of information that make for fun discussion in your classroom. The content is most appropriate for high school, but some middle school educators and students might benefit as well.

Details

Audience	9–12 history educators, students
Type	audio
Resource type	curriculum
Source/Author	Theodore P. Capkanis
Location	Kansas City, MO
Source URL	http://talkinghistory.oah.org

Discovery Atlas

http://dsc.discovery.com/convergence/atlas/podcast/podcast.html

Description

Based on its amazing high-definition TV series, Discovery Atlas provides a video look at the people and culture from amazing places around the globe. The video podcasts are presented as full segments in standard format that can be played on any MP3 player that supports video.

Sample Topics

> New York's Chinatown

> China Revealed

> Brazil Revealed

> Italy Revealed

> Australia Revealed

Classroom Applications

There are few more powerful images and insightful perspective than those offered by Discovery Channel in this series. Stunning in HD, the episodes translate well to the smaller format of iPods and other video players. The site features maps and other background—including a game called *Atlas Quest*—that helps you extend and enrich discussions of the places featured in the series.

Details

Audience	K–12, higher education students, educators, general public
Type	video
Resource type	instructional
Frequency	archived
Source/Author	Discovery Channel
Source URL	http://dsc.discovery.com/convergence/atlas/atlas.html

National Geographic

www.nationalgeographic.com/podcasts/

Description

National Geographic offers a variety of podcasts focusing on history, science, and geography. *National Geographic News* is a weekly broadcast of interviews, quizzes, and science and nature news. *National Geographic World Talk* features interviews with explorers, photographers, and other interesting people from around the world.

Sample Podcasts

> National Geographic News

> Traveler Magazine's Walks of a Lifetime

> National Geographic World Talk

> Wild Chronicles

> Best of National Geographic Magazine

> Dog Whisperer

> National Geographic Minutes

Classroom Applications

Very high quality audio and video podcasts from an unimpeachable source. The podcasts from National Geographic are supported by online resources and offer some very compelling material for geography, nature studies, and science classes. The *National Geographic Minute*, new each Friday, offers a quick 60-second update excellent for current events or current geography/science presentations. Challenge your students to sample all the podcasts on the site, though. There are many nuggets you'll find useful!

Details

Audience	K–12, higher education students, educators, general public
Type	audio/video
Resource type	instructional
Frequency	archived
Source/Author	National Geographic editors
Source URL	www.nationalgeographic.com

History Podcast

www.historyonair.com/archive.htm

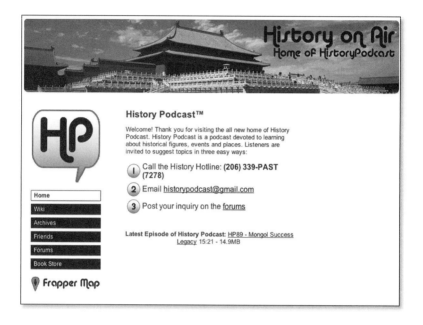

Description

A wide and deep library of short podcasts on key historical figures. You'll find perspectives on everyone from Lady Godiva to Stonewall Jackson hidden in the archives. Each segment focuses on the historical impact of key figures and offers a discussion about how these figures fit into the bigger picture in politics, society and life.

Sample Topics

> Godzilla

> Clara Barton

> Battle of Blair Mountain

Classroom Applications

I'm not sure if Godzilla is a historical figure, but I found a podcast focusing on this mythical creature and the impact of the films on culture on the history podcast site. Of course, most of the archives are more traditionally focused, but I liked this one, which is produced by students at the University of Kansas.

Details

Audience	9–12 students, educators
Type	audio
Resource type	instructional
Frequency	varies, a series
Source/Author	Jason Watts
Source URL	www.historyonair.com

History According to Bob

www.summahistorica.com

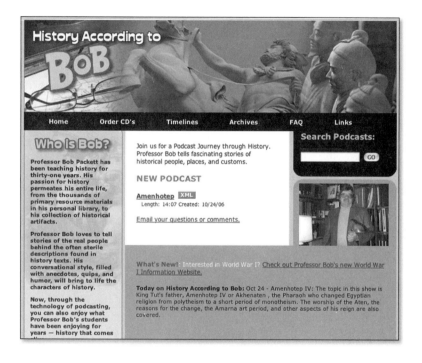

Description

Professor Bob Packett presents stories of real people and enlivens discussions about historical figures. Each podcast contains background information, anecdotes and a scattering of wit.

This 31-year veteran educator presents a current podcast for free, and archives are available for purchase on a CD.

Sample Topics

> Pirate Jean Lafitte

> Battle of Granicus River

> Road to Revolution

> History Theater

Classroom Applications

I like these podcasts because they're conversational and present historical events in a podcast that feels like you're sitting across from Professor Bob, hearing a story. The delivery style of the podcaster is lively and holds your attention. This podcast is an excellent way to introduce historical concepts and key figures, or to allow students a different perspective on events than their more traditional textbooks present.

Details

Audience	K–12 students
Type	audio
Resource type	instructional
Frequency	weekly
Source/Author	Bob Packett
Source URL	www.summahistorica.com

Free Government Information (FGI)

http://freegovinfo.info/node/174/

Description

This site offers a collection of podcasts from a variety of federal and state government officials and agencies. You can hear the president's weekly radio address, or listen in on selected town meetings.

Sample Topics

> President's Weekly Radio Address

> House Democrats Podcast Feed

> House Republicans Podcast Feed

> Committee on Government Reform (Democrats)

> Senator Barak Obama's Weekly Podcast

> California Governor's Weekly Address

Classroom Applications

The perfect dashboard for monitoring state and local government information. The site also includes such diverse information as the Voice of America broadcast and a cool daily feature, called *Profile America*, from the census bureau.

Details

Audience	K–12 educators and technology coordinators
Type	audio
Resource type	news and events
Frequency	weekly
Source/Author	U.S. Government
Source URL	http://freegovinfo.info

White House RSS Feeds and Podcasts

www.whitehouse.gov/rss/

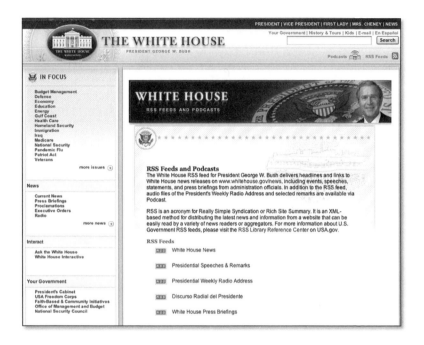

Description

The White House delivers podcasts and news feeds of news releases, events, speeches and press briefings from administration officials.

Sample Topics

> Presidential Speeches & Remarks

> President's Weekly Radio Address

> Discurso Radial del Presidente

> White House Press Briefings

> Barney Cam (Video)

Classroom Applications

Straight from the source, the White House offers a variety of audio and video podcasts updated weekly. The Web site offers helpful links and background information too. Most appropriate for government and civics classes.

Details

Audience	K–12 educators and technology coordinators
Type	audio/video
Resource type	news and events
Frequency	varies
Source/Author	U.S. Government
Location	Washington, DC
Source URL	www.whitehouse.gov/rss/

CHAPTER 10

Podcasts for Fine Arts

Tour a museum, hone your photography skills, plan a major theatrical production

Podcasting and vodcasting lend themselves incredibly well to sharing information, ideas, artwork and music. The format allows students to get new audiences for their own work, get feedback from their peers, and sample visual and audio media from sources both obscure and commonplace.

In this chapter, you'll find sites that let you tour museums, sample what's needed for a high school musical, listen to samples from a very enthusiastic middle school band class, and more.

Philadelphia Museum of Art

www.philamuseum.org/podcast/

Description

Art tours, exhibition notes, interviews and collection updates are just a few elements of this podcast presented by the Philadelphia Museum of Art. The *Art Tours*, such as a stroll through a Chagall exhibit or a stroll through Latrobe furniture, are interesting both as a tour guide on-site, and as a study guide for important works featured.

Sample Topics

> Arts and Armor

> Historic America

> Latrobe: Suite of Furniture

Classroom Applications

It might seem odd to include a museum podcast archive in this section, but these recordings shed lots of insight into how art is displayed and interpreted. There are many short tours and features contained in the Philadelphia Museum's podcast archives and a wealth of other information, including activities, on the museum's Web site. One activity that makes sense with this podcast content is an artwork scavenger hunt where students attempt to find images of sculptures and other artwork talked about in each segment. Another activity would be to collect and analyze the jargon used in selected tours and apply those descriptions and terms to art in your school or community.

Details

Audience	K–12 students
Type	audio
Resource type	instructional
Frequency	varies, a series
Source/Author	Philadelphia Museum
Location	Philadelphia, PA
Source URL	www.philamuseum.org

The Composers Notebook

http://nolanschmit.com/site/the_composers_notebook/
the_composers_notebook.html

Description

Conducting, composition and music instruction, all through the eyes of Nolan Schmit, a composer-educator who graduated with his Master of Music degree from the University of Nebraska–Lincoln in 2003. The podcast includes snippets of performances, analysis of instructional techniques, and interviews with composers and performers from obscure to professional.

Sample Topics

> Composers and Coffee (series)

> Revising and Performing

> Planning a Work for Concert Band

Classroom Applications

This podcast, for higher-level music students, ranges from simple interviews to discussions of very complex techniques and methodology related to the creation and performance of music. Particularly interesting are the *Composers and Coffee* interviews with jazz guitarists, pianists, trumpet players and others—all who make their livings performing or composing music. Students can get a good perspective on the creative process and the realities of the music business as they listen to some very good music.

Details

Audience	9–12 students, music educators
Type	audio
Resource type	instructional
Frequency	varies
Source/Author	Nolan Schmit
Location	Lincoln, NE
Source URL	http://nolanschmit.com

Your High School Musical

http://yourhighschoolmusical.podomatic.com

Description

Disney's *High School Musical* (the movie) is now sweeping stages, both school and professional, across the country. This podcast presents updates on the movie, as well as the seven licensed schools that will be performing the theatrical versions of *High School Musical* in 2007.

Sample Topics

> › Ready to Do Your Own High School Musical?

> › Productions in Your Area

Classroom Applications

If you're looking for next year's theatrical production for your school, this might be a good place to begin. Music Theater International recently released the rights for production. The podcast contains news, updates on the actors in the Disney movie, and other tips that can help get your students excited about the production—or just pick up some podcasting tips.

Details

Audience	K–12 students
Type	audio
Resource type	instructional
Frequency	varies, a series
Source/Author	Steve Butler
Location	Atlanta, GA
Source URL:	http://yourhighschoolmusical.com

Digital Photography Tips from the Top Floor

itpc://www.tipsfromthetopfloor.com/wp-rss2.php

Description

From tips about image composition to using low-end to high-end cameras, Tips from the Top Floor offers straight-to-the-point tips and techniques for creating and editing digital images. This 2005 and 2006 Podcast Award-winning show offers a support Web site that includes a searchable archive and is a rare glimpse into the expertise of a working professional photographer.

Sample Topics

> › Shooting Natural Portraits

> › Light, Light, Light

> › Burst Trick: Taking Pictures Without Camera Shake

Classroom Applications

This podcast offers tips and techniques for beginners and professionals alike. The tone is light and often irreverent, so it's likely a good solution for teachers preparing lessons or looking for tips to share with everyone from school newspaper reporters to the photography club. Particularly good are the "101 Ways to Improve Your Photography" (it's actually about 50) as a support resource found on the podcast's Web site.

Details

Audience	K–12, higher education educators, technology coordinators
Type	audio
Resource type	instructional, blog
Frequency	about once a week
Source/Author	Chris Marquardt
Source URL	www.tipsfromthetopfloor.com

NACOcast

www.nac-cna.ca/en/multimedia/podcasts/

Description

Host Christopher Millard (principal bassoon, National Arts Centre Orchestra) uses this podcast for commentary about orchestral music and updates along with some behind-the-scenes interviews from the National Arts Centre in Ottawa, Canada.

Sample Topics

> The Oboe

> Hungarian Celebration

> A Fifth of Quarrington

> Brahms

> Beethoven, Bernardi, Prystawski

> It's a Living (Life in a Professional Orchestra)

Classroom Applications

This podcast presents a commentary useful to students studying music and/or anyone who just loves orchestral presentations. The podcasts each feature snippets of music and a topic. One podcast, for example, focuses on the oboe—from how to make reeds to the development of the instrument. The content is high level, but music aficionados will appreciate the discussion.

Details

Audience	9–12 students, music educators
Type	audio
Resource type	instructional
Frequency	varies
Source/Author	Christopher Millard
Location	National Arts Centre Ottawa, Canada
Source URL	www.nac-cna.ca/en/

ARTSEDGE

http://artsedge.kennedy-center.org/explore/lll.cfm

Description

ARTSEDGE, a product of the wizards at the John F. Kennedy Center for Performing Arts, offers a variety of podcasts and other media following the theme of look, listen, learn. Each segment offers background resources, lesson plans, and notations about standards-based instruction.

Sample Topics

> A Dancer's Journey: Martha Graham Brand

> Brave No World

> Listen to the Nightingale

> Sound of China

> Stormy Weather

Classroom Applications

ARTSEDGE provides free, standards-based teaching materials, like these podcasts, for use in the classroom. Their Web site offers professional development resources, student materials, and guidelines for arts-based instruction and assessment. Each timeless and topical session focuses on a different type of music, performance or dance. One of my favorites, called *Sounds of China* (http://artsedge.kennedy-center.org/content/3899/), walks students through background and information about Chinese music and compares and contrasts it to Western music.

Details

Audience	K–12 students
Type	audio
Resource type	instructional
Frequency	varies, a series
Source/Author	The Kennedy Center, MarcoPolo project
Source URL	http://artsedge.kennedy-center.org

SFMOMA Artcasts

www.sfmoma.org/education/edu_podcasts.html

Description

The San Francisco Museum of Modern Arts' podcast series is designed as a companion to the museum's exhibits but also provides a fascinating look at artists, writers, curators and visitors with recorded responses to artwork and exhibitions.

Sample Topics

> **Voices from the Collection.** Kevin Conger and Mark Jensen of Jensen & Macy Architects discuss their winning design for the SFMOMA Sculpture Garden competition, and sculptor Robert Arneson talks about his love affair with clay.

> **Exhibition Highlights.** Art historian Patricia Albers shares the story of Tina Modotti and Edward Weston's partnership, and British artist Joshua Sofaer previews SFMOMA Scavengers, a citywide scavenger hunt and its subsequent exhibition.

> **Guest Interviews.** San Francisco-based recording artists Matmos offer a creative response to the work of Matthew Barney.

> **Gallery Exploration.** Art historian and Tina Modotti biographer Patricia Albers narrates a companion audio guide for Mexico as Muse: Tina Modotti and Edward Weston.

Classroom Applications

If you'd like to teach your students more about art appreciation, description and ways to enjoy art more, these podcasts are a good beginning. Couple them with images of the collections from SFMOMA's Web site for a virtual museum experience. You can also use this as a model for creating a podcast of an online or offline gallery of artwork created by your students.

Details

Audience	K–12, higher education students, educators, general public
Type	audio
Resource type	instructional
Frequency	monthly
Source/Author	San Francisco Museum of Modern Art
Location	San Francisco, CA
Source URL	www.sfmoma.org

smARThistory

http://smarthistory.org/blog/

Description

This video podcast focuses on using images and technology to teach art and art history. The episodes show some stunning images and helpful banter between two art historians—Beth Harris and Steven Zucker—from the History of Art Faculty in the Fashion Institute of Technology in New York, NY.

Sample Topics

> Rembrandt's Self-Portrait from 1660

> David's Death of Socrates, 1787

> Gerard David's Madonna and Child with Angels

Classroom Applications

You and your students can learn about art and art history from the experts as you follow along with video and still–frame illustrations during each podcast. The content of the shows is very high level and contains very focused analyses of artwork, architecture, and more. This podcast is also one of a relatively few enhanced podcasts that offers audio timed with image presentation—complete with on-screen annotation and pointers.

Details

Audience	10–12 students, higher education students, art educators
Type	enhanced video
Resource type	instructional
Frequency	varies, a series
Source/Author	Beth Harris and Steven Zucker
Location	Fashion Institute of Technology, New York City, NY
Source URL	http://smarthistory.org/blog/

Freedom Band

www.myfreedomband.org/news.htm

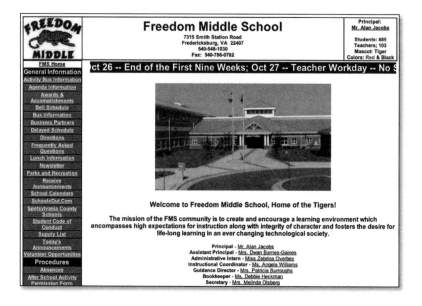

Description

This podcast combines local band news from Freedom Middle School (Fredericksburg, VA), student performances and musings from the highly creative educator, Chris Hoovler.

Sample Topics

> Student Solos

> Class Performances

> Special Events

> Contests

Classroom Applications

Great for budding band students, this podcast is presented by a middle school band director and educator and offers snippets of student music, contests, and much more. A good model for your own music program, or an inspiration for students.

Details

Audience	middle, high school students and educators
Type	audio
Resource type	instructional
Frequency	varies
Source/Author	Chris Hoovler, Freedom Middle School
Location	Fredericksburg, VA
Source URL	www.myfreedomband.org

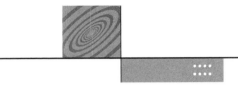

CHAPTER 11

Podcasts for Physical Education, Health, and Wellness

Keeping fit and learning more about who you are and how your body works

We're lucky that there are thousands of doctors, nurses, medical organizations, gyms, spas, and health organizations eager to share information. Many realize the power of podcasting to get their important messages across.

This chapter hints at the wide variety of podcasts you'll find to help you and your students explore health and wellness issues. You'll find podcasts that range from weekly updates from the U.S. government to fitness and weight training tips from a local fitness guru.

Healthcare 411

www.healthcare411.org

Description

This podcast features current news and information from the Agency for Healthcare Research and Quality (AHRQ), part of the U.S. Department of Health and Human Services. The segments are topical and present updates on research and development in health, healthcare, and medical research.

Sample Topics

> HIT is Used to Treat Pressure Ulcers

> Medical Intern Work Hours and Medical Errors

> Health Care for Minority Women

> Nurse-led Care Improves Heart Patient Recovery

> Obesity Surgery

> Second-hand Smoke

Classroom Applications

It's difficult sometimes to find current and credible information about health trends and issues to share with students. The AHRQ is part of the U.S. Department of Health and Human Services and its podcast offers excellent newscasts with background that can drive discussion and understanding in your classroom. Each segment also contains a public service announcement. As with any content you use, be sure to screen the podcasts from this site before airing to students in Grades 9–12.

Details

Audience	9–12 and higher education educators, general public
Type	audio
Resource type	instructional
Frequency	weekly
Source/Author	AHRQ (Agency for Healthcare Research and Quality), a unit of the U.S. Department of Health and Human Services
Source URL	www.healthcare411.org

UNICEF Podcast

www.unicef.org/videoaudio/video_podcast.html

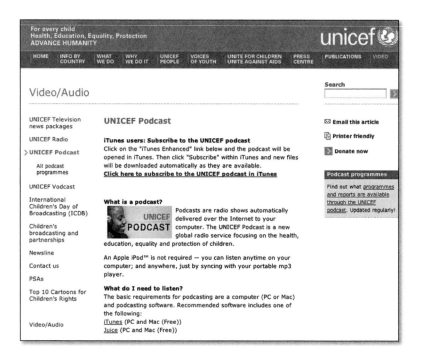

Description

This podcast features a global radio program focused on education, health, equality, and the protection of children. The segments discuss social issues from around the world and often include on-the-scene interviews in countries in great need.

Sample Topics

> Digital Diary: A Youth Anti-violence Activist in the Philippines Tells Her Story

> Protecting the Main Water Source of Grand Comore Island from Future Volcanic Eruptions

> Cameroon: Peer Educators Help Fight HIV/AIDS

> Displaced Children At Risk in Jaffna

Classroom Applications

These podcasts will help you knock down classroom walls by providing a perspective and a reality check relating to children around the world. The podcasts are typically short (3 minutes) and are useful in discussions of world events, history, sociology, cultural anthropology, or projects on health and health issues. Be sure to preview issues before using with younger students as some convey images and content that could be disturbing.

Details

Audience	6–12, higher education students, educators, general public
Type	audio
Resource type	instructional
Frequency	weekly
Source/Author	UNICEF
Location	varies
Source URL	www.unicef.org

Office of National Drug Control Policy

www.whitehousedrugpolicy.gov/podcast/rss/

Description

Information, interviews, and conference proceedings from the U.S. government agency that establishes policies and objectives for the nation's drug control programs.

Sample Topics

> Teens, Technology, and Drugs: An Inside Look

> Release of the U.N. World Drug Report

> Risky Behaviors

Classroom Applications

This podcast can help you gain valuable insight into what's new (newer than what's in your textbook) in efforts to identify, target, and eradicate drug abuse in the U.S. Resources such as the U.N. World Drug Report can be incredibly useful to students seeking resources for reports and projects. The target reports, such as a recent report on Teen Drug use, can also help extend the content in your health and science texts.

Details

Audience	K–12, higher education students, educators, general public
Type	audio
Resource type	instructional
Frequency	varies
Source/Author	Office of National Drug Control Policy
Source URL	www.whitehousedrugpolicy.gov

Exertrack

www.exertrack.com/exertrackmp3/exertrack_podcasts_default.htm

Description

A library of podcasts that provide listeners with specific instructions for proper form and coaching for common exercises for the abs, arms, chest, and legs.

Sample Topics

> › Crunches

> › Cable Triceps Extension

> › Dumbbell Biceps Curl

> › Dumbbell Chest Press

Classroom Applications

These short podcasts might provide motivation and emphasize good form as students work to be healthier, build muscle, and lose weight. The free podcasts can be augmented by the site's commercial Exertrack software and Exertrack network (online) used to track progress. If you like the style and format of these podcasts, you might challenge your students to make their own!

Details

Audience	K–12, higher education students, educators, general public
Type	audio
Resource type	instructional
Frequency	weekly
Source/Author	Marina Kamen
Source URL	www.exertrack.com

CHAPTER 12

Podcasts for Foreign Language

Podcasts that help you learn and communicate around the world

The podcast medium is extremely well suited to the study of foreign language. Because the content is presented in a format that can be easily stored and replayed for emphasis or study, language learning or language development may be accelerated for audio (or visual) learners.

In this chapter, you'll find just a sampling of language learning sites. Because teaching methods differ as widely as the languages they foster, it makes sense for you to check out these sites, and then look for those podcasts that better mirror your own teaching and learning methods.

A Spoonful of Russian

http://speakrussian.blogspot.com

Description

This site dedicated to Russian conversational language focuses on everyday conversations and everyday topics, like ordering food or addressing other people.

Sample Topics

> Happy Birthday

> Getting Around

Classroom Applications

Everyone is always looking for resources to augment instruction as more students who are learning, and speaking, languages other than English appear in classrooms. This site offers well-organized, refreshing content. The podcaster even recruits members of her family, like her daughters, to help her out.

Details

Audience	K–12 language teachers, ESL educators
Type	audio
Resource type	instructional
Frequency	weekly
Source/Author	Natalia Worthington
Location	New Orleans, LA
Source URL	http://speakrussian.blogspot.com

ChinesePod

www.chinesepod.com

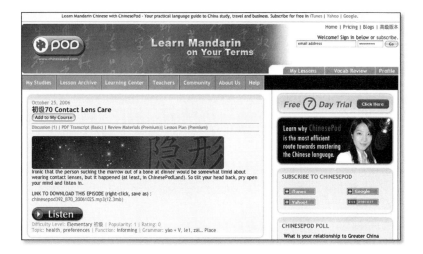

Description

ChinesePod is a resource for the study of Mandarin, combining podcasting, online learning materials, and a global community of fellow students. The podcasts require a subscription and a nominal shareware fee, but the quality and level of resources, access to message boards and lesson plans make this a good value for the money.

Sample Topics

> No, Thank You

> What is this called?

> Lost Luggage

Classroom Applications

This site offers hundreds of lessons, in addition to a very "listenable" podcast filled with instruction in Mandarin Chinese. The site delivers basic instruction and premium features, such as flashcards, word banks, etc., at a low cost. Visit the site's About Us page for several lessons available for free download. A free trial for the entire resource site is also available.

Details

Audience	K–12 educators
Type	audio
Resource type	instructional
Frequency	daily
Source/Author	varies
Source URL	www.chinesepod.com

Trying to Learn Spanish

www.tryingtolearnspanish.blogspot.com

Trying to Learn Spanish Web Site

A blog and podcast about "Trying to Learn Spanish". A discussion of many of the resources available. Comments and reviews on immersion language schools, tapes and CDs to learn Spanish, grammer books, websites, podcasts, Internet radio and more. To automatically download with your RSS downloader set feed to:
http://feeds.feedburner.com/TryingToLearnSpanishPodcast

WEDNESDAY, JANUARY 25, 2006

podcast #16, audio magazines

podcast #16, audio magazines

(link to this episode of the podcast)

ThinkSpanish audio magazine

(buy packs of ThinkSpanish audio magazine)

Puerta del Sol audio magazine

LoMásTV website

Democracy Now! titulares en español

online pop-up dictionaries
Ultralingua (for the Mac & Windows)
Oxford Spanish Pop-up dictionary (for Windows only)

please email me at: learningspanish@gmail.com,

or leave your comments on this site

posted by Rich @ 4:26 PM   16 comments

16 Comments:

About Me

Name:
Rich
Location:
Colorado, US

View my complete profile

Previous Posts

- podcast #15, vocabulary flash cards
- podcast #14, Instant Immersion Spanish Deluxe
- podcast #13, Destinos, Textbooks, & Dictionaries
- podcast #12, Immersion Language Schools II
- podcast #11, reading books to learn Spanish
- podcast #10, Intermediate Grammar Books
- podcast #9, Grammar Books
- podcast #8A, Immersion Language Schools IA
- podcast #8, Immersion Language Schools I

Description

A series of podcasts about learning the Spanish language from a podcaster who believes a variety of resources for learning a language is better than any one method. Each podcast archive covers curriculum ideas and a litany of links, books, other podcasts and URLs to help beginning learners get a full grasp of the Spanish language.

Sample Topics

> Grammar Books

> Immersion Language Schools

> Audio Magazines

Classroom Applications

While the production of this podcast isn't terrific, the methodology and content is. The host delivers instruction at a slow pace, suitable for beginning learners, and often tips the listener to other resources (podcasts and books, for example) that he's found useful in learning the language.

Details

Audience	K–12 educators, ESL teachers, 9–12 students
Type	audio
Resource type	instructional
Frequency	varies
Source/Author	Rich B.
Location	Colorado
Source URL	www.tryingtolearnspanish.blogspot.com

Brazilian Portuguese Podcast

http://brportuguesepod.podbean.com/feed/

Description

Over 200 million people worldwide speak Portuguese. It's not limited to Portugal—it's the official language of five countries, including Brazil. This very simply produced podcast, delivered by a native speaker, focuses on teaching beginning Brazilian Portuguese, including slang, common expressions, pronunciation, Brazilian culture, and differences between Portuguese and Brazilian Portuguese.

Sample Topics

> Personal Pronouns

> Months and Seasons

> Polite Words

Classroom Applications

The lessons presented in this podcast include music in Portuguese and everyday conversational phrases. André Barbosa has also listed lots of (clean) Web links from YouTube.com featuring native speakers so you can hear how different dialects sound.

Details

Audience	K–12 educators
Type	audio
Resource type	instructional
Frequency	varies
Source/Author	André Barbosa
Location	San Paolo, Brazil
Source URL	http://brportuguesepod.podbean.com

Japanese Class

www.kjls.or.jp/podcast/classes/lessons/lessons.html

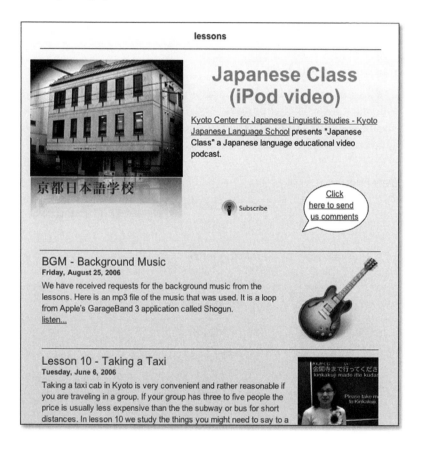

Description

Basic conversational Japanese taught entirely in Japanese with English subtitles. This immersion approach ensures quick mastery of simple direct conversations about everyday issues, like purchasing items or ordering food.

Sample Topics

> Taking a Taxi

> Conversation at a Bus Stop

> Asking About Locations

Classroom Applications

This site presents an immersion approach with all lessons in Japanese with English subtitles. Some students found this method more effective, some more distracting, so you'll have to test this one out. The site is well organized and, because it's primarily in Japanese, is good for ESL students.

Details

Audience	K–12 educators
Type	video
Resource type	instructional
Frequency	varies
Source/Author	Japanese Center for Linguistic Study
Location	Kyoto, Japan
Source URL	www.kjls.or.jp

FrenchPodClass

www.frenchpodclass.com

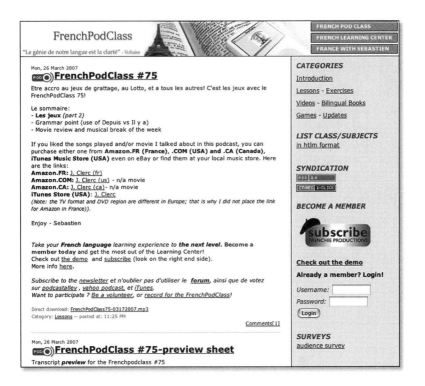

Description

The FrenchPodClass is offered by a native French speaker who's not an educator, but who is dedicated to spreading the French language through stories and instruction. The host is studying to be a Grade K–3 educator and offers very basic, but well organized content.

Sample Topics

> BilingualBook

> Elections

Classroom Applications

With more than 65 podcasts under his belt, Sebastien does a credible job sharing insights and vocabulary in French. His podcasts often offer music, listener questions, and humorous stories. The podcast is very good for beginning learners or those who want to continue their language studies. His methodology includes speaking each sentence in English and French. The pace is a bit quick, but not so quick as to lose the listener.

Details

Audience	9–12 educators, students
Type	audio
Resource type	instructional
Frequency	weekly
Source/Author	Sebastien, Frenchie Productions
Source URL	www.frenchieproductions.com

ESL Podcast

www.eslpod.com

Description

This podcast was designed specifically for ESL teachers and contains a wealth of content, presented in bite-sized segments, by a volunteer team of experienced ESL educators. The more than 60 activities and segments are divided by topic—English Café, Travel, and so forth. Most content on the site is free, but the site offers premium content, like learning guides and cultural notes and questions, for a small fee.

Sample Topics

> English Café: Houston

> A Generation Gap

> Shopping for Shoes

> Text Messaging

Classroom Applications

Each podcast comes with a learning guide that helps guide teachers and students through the segments. User questions and guest interviews help keep this podcast lively. If you're an ESL educator, this site could become a welcome resource for classroom preparation, student review, and lesson ideas.

Details

Audience	K–12 educators, 9–12 students, higher education students
Type	audio
Resource type	instructional
Frequency	weekly
Source/Author	varies
Source URL	www.eslpod.com

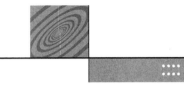

CHAPTER 13

Podcasts for News and Research

Keeping in touch via podcast with the digital planet

Podcasts that feature news, events and information for research are a lot like radio. Usually very professionally crafted and produced, these podcasts feature local, regional, national and international news presented in bite-sized segments. Unlike radio, though, you can hone in on exactly the type of news you'd like to hear and, because it's time-shifted, determine exactly when you want to hear it.

Most of the big news organizations, such as CNN, ABC, and Reuters, offer a range of podcasts focused on everything from top stories to in-depth coverage of current issues. The podcasts in this chapter include a starter set of podcasts produced by news organizations in the main media and in technology. There are plenty more, of course. Search news and podcasts to see some of them.

National Public Radio

www.npr.org/rss/podcast/podcast_directory.php

Description

National Public Radio (NPR) offers hundreds of podcasts including recent news, discussions about major issues, interviews, music, and much more. Once a month, NPR features *NPR: Playback* where they flash back to events of 25 years and re-air excerpts from their archives.

Sample Topics

> Future Tense: Daily Program Chronicles the Social Impact of Technology.

> Radio Without Borders: A Variety of Very Diverse Music from Austin, Texas

> KQED's Perspectives: A Series of Daily Commentaries By the Listeners of a Northern California Public Radio Station.

Classroom Applications

As with their radio broadcasts, the NPR podcasts tend to be much richer in background, thought, and intelligent conversation than their mass-media counterparts. The *Memorable Moments* podcast, a yearly summary of events, is a perfect way to begin discussion in history, current events, and sociology classes. Music programming is appropriate for studies of world geography and culture, as a writing starter, or in music classes. Other programming can also be used as background for lessons in history, economics and just about any other subject. The Web site is well organized with podcasts categorized for easy access.

Details

Audience	K–12, higher education students, educators, general public
Type	audio
Resource type	instructional
Frequency	varies
Source/Author	NPR staff and guests
Location	varies
Source URL	www.npr.org

CNN

www.cnn.com/services/podcasting/

Description

CNN offers top stories, replays of on-air broadcasts, special event programming, news digests and more. Its *News Update* is presented hourly and the daily *Now in the News* offers top stories and light background information to help you keep up with current events.

Sample Topics

> Now in the News—Commuter Edition

> CNN Daily

> All Access—Backstage Pass

> In Case You Missed It

Classroom Applications

Like the network, CNN's podcasts present well-written, timely and informative content. Teachers and students can use the podcast content to stay up on current events, or deep-dive into a topic by listening to multiple sources for varied perspectives. One nugget that you shouldn't miss—*CNN Student News*—a ten-minute, commercial-free daily program designed to bring news stories to middle and high school students. The program offers background material and teacher's guides too.

Details

Audience	K–12, higher education students, educators, general public
Type	audio and video
Resource type	informational
Frequency	daily
Source/Author	Cable News Network (CNN)
Location	varies
Source URL	www.cnn.com

The New York Times

www.nytimes.com/ref/multimedia/podcasts.html

Description

Podcasts from this credible news source cover a huge variety of topics including current news, science, technology, health, advertising, sports, books and music. The podcast segments are typically short (most about five minutes) and are designed for a broad consumer market.

Sample Topics

> Tech Talk

> TimesSelect Sample

> Front Page

> Theater Update

> Restaurant Update

Classroom Applications

Daily podcasts like *Front Page* are great for current events discussions in class. Don't miss *The Ethicist*, a discussion about reader's questions on ethical issues, if you need topics for discussion, writing or debate. Most podcasts are columns read by their authors. Content from The New York Times is useful in social studies classes, as writing idea starters, or for research on current topics.

Details

Audience	K–12, higher education students, educators, general public
Type	audio
Resource type	informational
Frequency	daily
Source/Author	The New York Times
Source URL	www.nytimes.com

ABC News

http://abcnews.go.com/technology/podcasting/

Description

ABC News brings its on-air video programming to video podcast players everywhere. From *Good Morning America* segments to special events, you'll find a huge library of podcast content on their Web site.

Sample Topics

> › World News Video Webcast

> › The Journalist and the Prisoner (Special Report)

> › Brian Ross Investigates

> › 20/20 in Touch

Classroom Applications

If it's video podcast content you want, ABC News is a leader. Its *ABC News Shuffle* presents short segments about the day's leading news items. Other segments are available featuring international, money, health, entertainment, sports, travel, and weather news. The site is well organized, so students can easily find vodcasts if they're doing research or want to stay in touch with current events. You might also choose several of the video podcasts from this site to use as a model—both in production and format—for your own school-based podcasts.

Details

Audience	K–12, higher education students, educators, general public
Type	video/audio
Resource type	informational
Frequency	daily
Source/Author	ABC News
Source URL	http://abcnews.go.com

CNET News

http://news.com.com/2030-11424_3-5845846.html

Description

Technology news, delivered in short blasts of technology data from a leader in news and information—CNET. Shows include daily updates, and topic-driven excerpts from CNET's television broadcasts.

Sample Topics

> Security Bites

> Coop's Corner

> Buzz Out Loud

> Reporters Round Table

Classroom Applications

If you want high-tech news, this is the place to start. The daily podcasts are witty, well written and packed with the latest news about everything from gadgets to games. Students and geeky teachers like me will love CNET's podcasts. The segments are excellent for technology coordinators and professional developers who want to keep an eye on what's happing in Silicon Valley as well.

Details

Audience	K–12, higher education students, educators, technology coordinators, professional development coordinators
Type	video
Resource type	informational
Frequency	varies
Source/Author	CNET Networks
Source URL	http://news.com.com

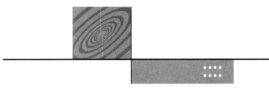

CHAPTER 14

Podcasts for Students by Students

*Students tell the story and shout it
to the world—one podcast at a time*

It was only a matter of time before educators and students began to become producers of podcast content. Schools are now podcasting their daily announcements, audio and video newsletters, class lectures, student-produced interview projects, and much more.

This chapter presents a quick sampling of a few diverse podcasts produced by schools around the globe. Listening to a few of them will give you an idea of the wide array of subjects covered, and production quality, that you'll find in the world of school podcasting. After sampling some of these, visit some of the online podcast directories (see appendix A) and search for more.

HanesMS.org—Sound Bytes

www.tclauset.org/wpa/

Description

Hanes Middle School in North Carolina offers podcasts of school newscasts, interviews, clubs and events. Its Web site offers podcasts for educators, too, discussing hot topics such as overloaded class schedules and ever-growing requirements for assessment. For students, there are newscasts, band concerts, and an online newspaper.

Sample Topics

> After-school Events and Activities

> Academics News

Classroom Applications

Students at Hanes Middle School not only produce a podcast, they do it very well. The podcasts are generally short—under 10 minutes. You and your students will enjoy listening to students at Hanes sharing their adventures and student-written dramatic presentations. The podcasts presented are a great model for your own school.

Details

Audience	Grade 6–8 students, educators
Type	audio
Resource type	news and events
Frequency	varies
Source/Author	Hanes Middle School students
Location	Winston-Salem, NC
Source URL	http://tclauset.org/wpa/?page_id=2

Radio WillowWeb

www.mpsomaha.org/willow/radio/

Description

A lively podcast presented by fifth graders—for students, by students. Each nicely produced segment contains vocabulary, student writing, facts about topics in the curriculum, and sometimes a feature called *Good Joke, Bad Joke.*

Sample Topics

> Endangered Animals

> Spotlight on Sound & Light

> Regarding the Revolution

> Life in the Colonies

> Know About Nebraska

> Take Off Your Shoes and Learn About Japan!

Classroom Applications

I know I'm not supposed to play favorites, but this podcast represents the best of the best in elementary podcast programs. Somehow, the students and teachers at Willowdale Elementary continue come up with well-written scripts and present information compelling enough for the most distracted student (or teacher). The mix of trivia and facts, writing and vocabulary, and snippets of fun will keep you and your students coming back for more. Be sure to check their Web site for tips, segment ideas, and links to other broadcasts to help you get even more ideas for your own podcasts.

Details

Audience	K–5 students, teachers, educators
Type	audio
Resource type	instructional
Frequency	varies
Source/Author	Willowdale Elementary School
Location	Omaha, NE
Source URL	www.mpsomaha.org/willow/

Jamestown Podcast

http://slapcast.com/users/Jamestown/

Jamestown Elementary XML

Jamestown Podcast

Thu, Jul 27 2006

Global Village Podcast- Portugal
Ms. Costa's class learned so many facts about Portugal. Listen to them as they share the many fun facts from Global Village!

LISTEN

Posted at 11:52 AM

Tue, Jul 25 2006

Global Village Podcast- Australia
Mrs. Adam's class presents you with lots of information on Australia that they learned while at Global Village Summit. Try to see if you learn some fun facts to share with your friends!

LISTEN

Description

These podcasts feature content from across the curriculum. Topic-focused segments feature writing, music and news from Jamestown Elementary classrooms. Notable segments include field trips (Jamestown Settlement), math problems, and discussions of literary works.

Sample Topics

> › Jamestown Settlement Field Trip Talk Show

> › Multiage Snow Poetry

> › Discovering the Zoo Online

> › Global Village Podcasts: Portugal

Classroom Applications

I love the interdisciplinary nature of these short podcasts. A recent challenge math problem took me 10 minutes to solve. Where are the fifth graders when I need them? Another highlight of these broadcasts is that the school involves lots of students so the podcasts don't get monotonous and even attention-challenged kids will enjoy them.

Details

Audience	Jamestown ES students and surrounding community
Type	audio
Resource type	news, events, curriculum
Frequency	weekly
Source/Author	Jamestown ES students
Location	Arlington, VA
Source URL	http://slapcast.com/users/Jamestown/

The Coulee Kids' Podcast

www.sdlax.net/longfellow/sc/ck/

School in the Coulee - Seventh Grade Curriculum Option - Longfellow Middle School

Longfellow Home   Coulee Home   News   Teacher Materials   Student Comments   Podcasting FAQ

The Coulee Kids' Podcast!

School in the Coulee students are proud to announce the 2006-2007 Coulee Kids' podcast! We welcome you to join us for an exciting year.

Listen to our Podcast by subscribing to our weekly update, and enjoy both the visual (photos and video) and audio.

Subscribe to this Podcast
1. Download iTunes, which is free and works on either a Mac or PC.
2. Once you have installed iTunes, subscribe to the Coulee Kids podcast. You can do this searching for the key word "Coulee" or click on the Coulee Kids link above.
3. Enjoy!

Download complete subscription instructions (PDF).

Participate in the Coulee Kids Virtual Poetry Slam.
Respond Today!

Description

This podcast showcases student work from Longfellow Middle School in La Crosse, WI. You never know what to expect—sometimes it's a rap about arthropods, another time a presentation of readings of students' work about beliefs and thoughts, the next day a math problem.

Sample Topics

> › iBelieve

> › Romeo and Juliet—A Literary Adaptation

> › Is It Just a Box?

> › Math—Thinking out of the Book

Classroom Applications

This podcast is another example of what happens when a creative faculty supports the use of technology across the curriculum. Segments are brief, but entertaining and show good planning and organization. Production value is good and the school loves to use original and royalty-free music to spice things up. A great place to find curriculum ideas, information for students, and a model for presenting curriculum content via podcast.

Details

Audience	Grade 6–8 students, parents, community
Type	audio
Resource type	news, events, curriculum
Frequency	weekly
Source/Author	Longfellow Middle School teachers and students
Location	La Crosse, WI
Source URL	www.lacrosseschools.com

Mabry Online.org Podcast Central

http://mabryonline.org/podcasts/

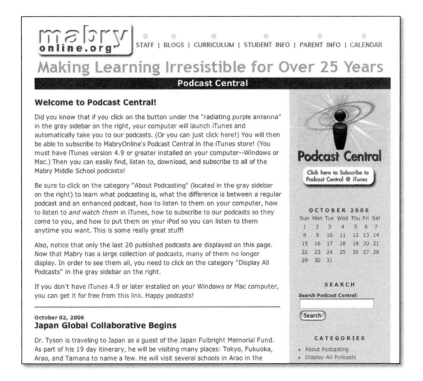

Description

A rapidly expanding library of podcasts covering curriculum activities, local school activities, even advertisements created by students about the school. Enhanced podcasts and video podcasts are also available.

Sample Topics

> Mr. Howard's Students Make Mabry Ad

> Japan Global Collaborative Begins

> Most Eggcellent Eggsperiment

> Film Festival

> Open House

Classroom Applications

The sheer volume of quality content for school and community set this site and the podcasts there apart from the rest. The production value is high and the Web site is well maintained. Click around the Web site and explore everything from board meetings to field trips to classroom activities. This is a school that really understands and embraces podcast technology and uses the media to keep parents involved, as well as to show student learning. This is a must-visit site if your school or district wants to integrate podcasting in every area of student learning and administration.

Details

Audience	6–8 students, educators, parents
Type	audio/video
Resource type	instructional
Frequency	varies
Source/Author	Mabry Middle School
Location	Cobb County, GA
Source URL	http://mabryonline.org

Broward County Public Schools

feed://www.browardschools.com/feed/podcast.xml

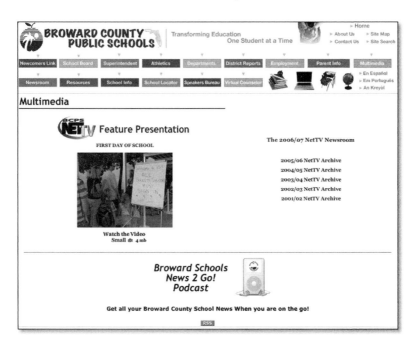

Description

The nation's sixth-largest school district takes podcasting district activities and school and student news to a new level. Monthly enhanced video podcasts are extraordinarily well produced and packed with video and audio.

Sample Topics

> › BCPS Update
>
> › News 2 Go!

Classroom Applications

I guess it's no surprise that one of the largest school districts in the nation would have video podcasts that rival mass-media networks in production value. What is surprising is the attention to detail and great diversity of information presented each month. Broward clearly knows how to tell its story and parents in the community, and others world-wide, get a very good picture of the wonderful things that happen in the district through the window of these video podcasts. This is the podcast to strive for—but don't get discouraged if you don't have all the video bells and whistles. Remember to focus on content first, flash second!

Details

Audience	K–12 students and educators, parents
Type	audio/video
Resource type	informational
Frequency	varies
Source/Author	Broward County Public Schools
Location	Broward County, FL
Source URL	www.browardschools.com

Nauset Public Schools Podcasts

http://feeds.feedburner.com/nausetpodcasts/

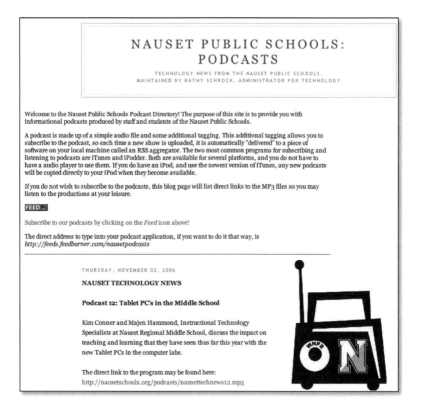

Description

Informational podcasts courtesy of Nauset Schools in Massachusetts. Technology administrator and guru Kathy Schrock hosts the podcast. Segments include interviews and ideas about using technology in the curriculum.

Sample Topics

> Nauset Educators Talk about Technology

> Kathy on the Road at Microsoft

> School District Technology Challenges

Classroom Applications

If you want short, information-packed perspectives about the latest technologies and how to integrate them into the curriculum, this podcast's for you. The host presents well-organized and produced podcasts that cover a wide range of technology topics.

Details

Audience	K–12 educators
Type	audio
Resource type	informational
Frequency	varies
Source/Author	Nauset Public Schools
Location	Orleans, MA
Source URL	http://nausetschools.org/podcasts/

Podkids Australia

http://podkids.com.au

Description

Podcast originating at Orange Grove Primary School in Western Australia. Each episode features curriculum reports, student interviews, and the Web site features show notes.

Sample Topics

> Save the Koala

> Kids Web Japan

> Trafkids

> Meerkats.com

Classroom Applications

You and your students will enjoy the curriculum reports in this podcast. Besides the charming Aussie accents, the podcast does a credible job presenting cross-disciplinary content. The show notes offer extended background and resources about each topic and step-by-step instructions for some activities.

Details

Audience	K–12 students
Type	audio
Resource type	instructional, informational
Frequency	daily
Source/Author	Orange Grove Primary School
Location	Perth, Western Australia
Source URL	http://podkids.com.au

Our City Podcast

http://learninginhand.com/OurCity/

Description

Produced by handheld computing guru and educator Tony Vincent, *Learning in Hand* podcasts focus on interdisciplinary projects. In *Our City*, students from around the globe are invited to submit a podcast about the city they live in.

Sample Topics

> Fabulous Phoenix (AZ)

> Caring about Killeen (TX)

> Glorious Glenview (IL)

> Cool Carlsbad (CA)

> Phantastic Philadelphia (PA)

Classroom Applications

Tony Vincent is well known for creative use of handheld technologies in his elementary classroom—now he helps other teachers create podcasts. Each *Our City* podcast includes notes, images, maps and background that make these truly memorable learning experiences. Be sure to check out the Meadow Lake, Saskatchewan, Canada, student broadcast for a well-polished, well-scripted, and informative educational production.

Details

Audience	K–12 students
Type	audio
Resource type	instructional, informational
Frequency	varies
Source/Author	schools around the world
Location	varies
Source URL	http://learninginhand.com

Cefn Fforest Primary Podcast

www.cefnfforest.podomatic.com

Description

A primary school podcast that features sing-alongs, stories, and cross-curricular exercises from students in K–4. The podcast, originating in South Wales, offers a rare glimpse into the curriculum, culture and school live in a very progressive Welsh community.

Sample Topics

> Colour Poems

> Visit the Iron Age Village at St. Fagans

> Arcimboldo

> Roald Dahl—The Twits

Classroom Applications

A great way to travel around the world without leaving your chair. These podcasts offer original music performances (the Welsh love to sing) and podcasts featuring classroom news and activities—many produced by the school's after-school podcasting club. The student interviews are informative and interesting. Be sure to listen to the fortnightly quiz.

Details

Audience	K–4
Type	audio
Resource type	instructional, informational
Frequency	daily
Source/Author	Cefn Fforest Primary School
Location	Blackwood, South Wales
Source URL	www.cefnfforest.podomatic.com

CHAPTER 15

Podcasts for
Higher Education

*A sampling of podcasts—from
lectures to news—from higher ed
institutions worldwide*

Probably because MP3 players are as common on college campuses as pizza delivery trucks, higher education began embracing podcasts for sharing lectures and other content more than three years ago. School-wide podcasting initiatives began to arise and nowadays you'll find plenty of good examples of higher education content on the Web.

In Massachusetts, for example, several professors at Tufts University, Boston College, Worcester State College, Emerson College, UMass-Lowell, Framingham State College, and MIT, as well as other colleges around the state, began independently creating podcasts of their courses three years ago. Class lecture podcasts became ubiquitous during the last year.

Stanford on iTunes U

http://itunes.stanford.edu

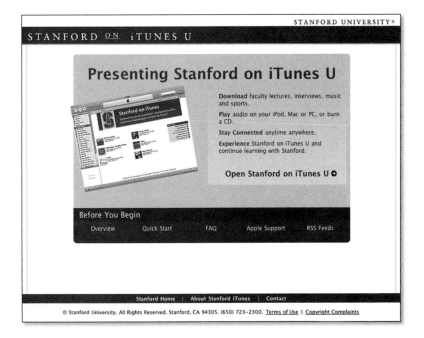

Description

From the heart of Silicon Valley, here's one of the first major universities to create an iTunes portal. Through this portal, you'll find podcast content about global issues, sports, books and authors, music, and faculty lectures.

Sample Topics

> Spiritual and Moral Inquiry in the Classroom: When and How is it Appropriate?

> Getting Ahead in School: How We Are Creating a Generation of Stressed-Out, Materialistic, and Miseducated Students

> Is Global Warming Real? Climate Change and Our Energy Future

> Presidential Politics and U.S. Foreign Policy

> Confronting Katrina: Race, Class, and Disaster in American Society: Foundations of Neglect

> Stress and Coping: What Baboons Can Teach Us

> Why Zebras Don't Get Ulcers

Classroom Applications

Stanford leads the way with two podcast sites. One designed for alumni features faculty lectures, music, sports news and more. The second, a restricted-access portal, contains coursework and course-based materials. The site was created as part of a program at Apple called iTunes U. More information can be found at www.apple.com/education/products/ipod/itunes_u.html.

Details

Audience	higher education students, educators, general public
Type	audio
Resource type	instructional
Frequency	varies
Source/Author	professors and students at Stanford University
Location	Stanford University, Stanford, CA
Source URL	http://itunes.stanford.edu

EDUCAUSE Connect—Conference Coverage

http://connect.educause.edu

Description

The EDUCAUSE conference brings together educators from all over the world to present and share ideas. Podcasts archives from the yearly EDUCAUSE conference offer a rich library of up-to-date information about technology, learning and teaching.

Sample Topics

> An Interview with Google's Vint Cerf

> Focus on Assessment

> An Interview with Penn State's Nancy Eaton

Classroom Applications

Every conference should follow EDUCAUSE's lead in sharing presentations via audio files and podcasts. These podcasts allow conference goers to review what they've heard, or those who couldn't make it to the conference a chance to stay informed. Sound quality varies, but the content can't be beat. If you have anything to do with an education conference, the presentation and organization of content on the organization's Web site are good models to follow.

Details

Audience	higher education students, faculty, administration
Type	audio
Resource type	instructional
Frequency	monthly
Source/Author	EDUCAUSE
Location	San Francisco, CA
Source URL	http://connect.educause.edu

University of Virginia Podcasts and Webcasts

www.virginia.edu/uvapodcast/

Description

The University of Virginia podcast features lectures, presentations, speeches and campus events interesting to a wide audience. There's also a link here with tips and techniques for beginning your own podcast or recording lectures at your school.

Sample Topics

> U.S. Census Director Speaks at Population Conference

> Space Flight: A Human Perspective

> More than the Score: The Physics of Football

Classroom Applications

The university does a very good job of keeping the podcast list current and the production quality of its podcasts is excellent. The Web site is also well organized with enough information presented about each podcast to help you make decisions about what to sample. This is another nice model for podcasting for universities and a good source of research information from UVA's campus.

Details

Audience	higher education students, faculty, administration
Type	audio
Resource type	instructional
Frequency	various
Source/Author	University of Virginia
Location	Charlottesville, VA
Source URL	www.virginia.edu

Screenshot Credits

Chapter 1 ›› Introduction to Podcasting

Pg. 10: © 2007 Apple, Inc. All rights reserved.

Pg. 19: © 2007 members of the Audacity development team.

Pg. 20: © 2007 Apple, Inc. All rights reserved.

Chapter 4 ›› General Education and Administration

Pg. 56: © Hamline University Graduate School of Education.
Reprinted with permission.

Pg. 58: © Learning.com. Reprinted with permission.

Pg. 60: © Dave LaMorte, Teaching for the Future Podcast. Reprinted with permission.

Pg. 62: © ASCD. Reprinted with permission.

Pg. 64: © 2007 Meredith Corporation. All rights reserved. Reprinted with permission.

Pg. 66: © 2007 Learning Point Associates, www.centerforcsri.org.
Reprinted with permission.

Pg. 68: © Learning Matters, Inc. Reprinted with permission.

Pg. 70: Reprinted with permission of Terry Freedman, www.ictineducation.org/db/
web2/ and http://web2booklet.blogspot.com; and Shawn Wheeler,
http://staffweb.peoriaud.k12.az.us/Shawn_Wheeler/podcast/.

Pg. 72: © Intelligenic. Reprinted with permission.

Pg. 74: © Learning and Teaching Scotland. Reprinted with permission.

Pg. 76: © Minneapolis Public Schools. Reprinted with permission.

Pg. 78: © Reed Business Information, a Division of Reed Elsevier, Inc.
Reprinted with permission of School Library Journal.

Chapter 5 ›› Podcasts About Education Technology

Pg. 82: © John Lien, Orange County Public Schools.
Reprinted with permission.

Pg. 84: © Apple, Inc. All rights reserved. Reprinted with permission.

Pg. 86: © 2007 David J. Malan, Harvard University, malan@post.harvard.edu.

Pg. 88: © K.P. King and M. Gura, Podcast for Teachers, Techpod,
http://www.podcastforteachers.org. Reprinted with permission.

Pg. 90: © Weblogs, Inc. All rights reserved. Reprinted with permission.

Pg. 92: Reprinted with permission of Tony Vincent's learninginhand.com.

Pg. 94: © 2007 Apple, Inc. All rights reserved. Reprinted with permission.

Pg. 96: Reprinted with permission of Christopher Essex, Instructional Consulting
Office, Indiana University School of Education.

Pg. 98: © International Society for Technology in Education.

Pg. 100: © Steve Sloan, founder and webmaster of Edupodder.com. Reprinted with
permission.

Chapter 6 ›› Podcasts for Mathematics

Pg. 104: © Mathtutor. All rights reserved. Reprinted with permission.

Pg. 106: © Jay Abramson, Department of Mathematics & Statistics, Arizona State University. Reprinted with permission.

Pg. 108: © Dan Bach, www.dansmath.com.

Pg. 110: Reprinted with permission of Christopher Frederick, www.mathgrad.com.

Pg. 112: Reprinted with permission of Chaim Goodman-Strauss and Kyle Kellams, University of Arkansas.

Chapter 7 ›› Podcasts for Science

Pg. 116: Reprinted with permission of Alice Few, creator of Astronomy a Go-Go! Podcast.

Pg. 118: © Jodrell Bank Observatory, the University of Manchester, UK.

Pg. 120: Reprinted with permission of www.TheWildClassroom.com.

Pg. 122: © The McGraw-Hill Companies. All rights reserved. Reprinted with permission.

Pg. 124: © AAAS, The Science Society. Reprinted with permission.

Pg. 126: © Rick Quarles, author of Science on the Wild Side Show Podcast. Reprinted with permission.

Pg. 128: © College of Earth and Mineral Sciences, Pennsylvannia State University. Reprinted with permission.

Pg. 130: © 2007 Scientific American, Inc. All rights reserved. Reprinted with permission.

Pg. 132: © NASA

Pg. 134: © Andrew Whitaker, creator of Instant Anatomy. Reprinted with permission.

Pg. 136: Reprinted with permission of Kyle Butler, the Brain Food Podcast, www.brainfoodpodcast.com.

Chapter 8 ›› Podcasts for English/Language Arts

Pg. 140: Reprinted with permission of Sabrina Weissler, host and producer of Childrensbookradio.com.

Pg. 142: © 2007 the Poetry Foundation. All rights reserved. Reprinted with permission.

Pg. 144: © Mark Kendall Anderson. Reprinted with permission.

Pg. 146: © Blog Relations Ltd. Reprinted with permission.

Pg. 148: © Disney Enterprises, Inc. Reprinted with permission.

Pg. 150: Reprinted with permission of The Princeton Review.

Pg. 152: Reprinted with permission of Reading Rockets, www.readingrockets.org.

Pg. 154: Reprinted with permission of Robert Diem and Roberto Rabbini, Creators of The Bob and Rob Show.

Chapter 9 ›› Podcasts for Social Science

Pg. 158: Reprinted with permission of Dave Fagg, creator of the iHistory Podcast Project.

Pg. 160: Reprinted with permission of David L. McCarthy and Brian K. Brunius, Thirteen/WNET New York, Educational Broadcasting Coproration, www.pbs.org/jimcrow/.

Pg. 162: © George Hageman, creator of the Military History Podcast. Reprinted with permission.

Pg. 164: © Organization of American Historians. Reprinted with permission.

Pg. 168: © 2007 National Geographic Society. Reprinted with permission.

Pg. 170: Reprinted with permission of historyonair.com.

Pg. 172: Reprinted with permission of Robert L. and Ruth Ellen Packett, History According to Bob or Summa.

Pg. 174: Reprinted with permission of Free Government Info. This work is licensed under a Creative Commons License.

Chapter 10 ›› Podcasts for Fine Arts

Pg. 180: Reprinted with permission of the Philadelphia Museum of Art.

Pg. 182: Reprinted with permission of Nolan Schmit, site creator.

Pg. 184: Reprinted with permission of Your High School Musical.

Pg. 186: Reprinted with permission of Chris Marquardt, Tips from the Top Floor.

Pg. 188: © National Arts Centre of Canada. Reprinted with permission.

Pg. 190: Reprinted with permission of ARTSEDGE, The John F. Kennedy Center for the Performing Arts.

Pg. 192: Reprinted with permission of the San Francisco Museum of Modern Art.

Pg. 194: © Dr. Beth Harris and Dr. Steven Zucker. Reprinted with permission.

Pg. 196: Reprinted with permission of Freedom Middle School.

Chapter 11 ›› Podcasts for Physical Education, Health, and Wellness

Pg. 200: © Heathcare411 Audio Series Podcasts, Agency for Healthcare Research and Quality, U.S. Department of Health and Human Services. Reprinted with permission.

Pg. 202: © UNICEF. Reprinted with permission.

Pg. 206: © Exertrack. Reprinted with permission.

Chapter 12 ›› Podcasts for Foreign Language

Pg 210: © Natalia Worthington. Reprinted with permission.

Pg 212: Reprinted with permission of chinesepod.com.

Pg 214: Reprinted with permission of Trying to Learn Spanish.

Pg 216: Reprinted with permission of André Augusto Souto Barbosa, owner, producer, and host of the Brazilian Portuguese Podcast.

Pg 218: © Kyoto Japanese Language School.

Pg 220: © Frenchie Productions. Reprinted with permission.

Pg 222: © Center for Educational Development, Inc. Reprinted with permission.

Chapter 13 ›› Podcasts for News and Research

Pg 226: © NPR. Reprinted with permission.

Pg 228: © CNN. Reprinted with permission.

Pg 230: © New York Times. Reprinted with permission.

Pg 232: © ABCNews Internet Ventures. Reprinted with permission.

Chapter 14 ›› Podcasts for Students by Students

Pg. 238: Reprinted with permission of Tom Clauset, Web Master and podcasting project coordinator at Hanes Middle School, http:www.hanesms.org.

Pg. 240: Reprinted with permission of Willowdale Elementary, Millard Public Schools.

Pg. 242: Reprinted with permission of Jamestown Elementary, Arlington Public Schools.

Pg. 244: © Coulee Kids. Reprinted with permission.

Pg. 246: © Tim Tyson and the staff and students of Mabry Middle School, Cobb County School District. Reprinted with permission.

Pg. 248: Reprinted with permission of Broward County Public Schools.

Pg. 250: Reprinted with permission of Nauset Public Schools, Orleans, MA; Michael B. Gradone, Superintendent and Kathleen Schrock, Podmaster.

Pg. 252: Reprinted with permission of Orange Grove Primary School.

Pg. 254: © Tony Vincent. Reprinted with permission.

Pg. 256: Reprinted with permission of Cefn Fforest Primary School.

Chapter 15 ›› Podcasts for Higher Education

Pg. 260: © The Board of Trustees of the Leland Stanford Junior University.

Pg. 262: © EDUCAUSE. Reprinted with permission.

Pg. 264: Reprinted with permission of the University of Virginia.

Podcast Directories

L ike most of the other content found on the Internet, new podcasts are added just about every minute. Directories spring up almost as frequently. In this chapter, you'll find a list of some of the more appropriate directories containing pathways to podcasts interesting and appropriate for the classroom. Most allow a keyword search and offer "one-click" subscriptions—automatically adding the podcast to your iTunes library or providing easy access to other podcatcher applications.

The Education Podcast Network: www.epnweb.org

Offers a well-organized subset of podcast content for teachers looking for ideas and resources for teaching and learning. Updated often, this directory should probably be your first stop for quality educational content.

Indiepodder: www.indiepodder.org

Originally set up by former MTV DJ Adam Curry, this site has grows as the quintessential example of how podcasting "works" in the commercial market. It features access to podcast aggregators (podcatchers) and a large directory of podcasts.

Podcast Alley: www.podcastalley.com

The Podcast Alley Web site has the most extensive listing of podcasts on the Web. It ranks podcasts based on the number of votes they receive each month. Don't limit yourself to the education category. Many applicable podcasts can be found in other categories! You can also perform a search.

Odeo: www.odeo.com

> An audio/video search engine. More than two million MP3 files from all over the web.

PODSCOPE: www.podscope.com

> An audio/video search engine that allows you to search the spoken word.

Yahoo! Podcasts: http://podcasts.yahoo.com

> Search podcasts series or for individual episodes by description and by tags listeners have assigned the podcasts. Also you can browse the categories. Listen right in your browser if you like. Subscribe using Yahoo! or copy and paste the RSS feed into iTunes.

iTunes Podcast Directory: iTunes application

> The newest version of iTunes has a built-in podcast directory. After launching iTunes, click the Podcasts icon in the Source panel. The categories are listed on the bottom left of the screen. You can also perform a search. iTunes is free software for Windows and Macintosh.

Educational Podcasting: www.recap.ltd.uk/podcasting/

> This UK directory lists podcasts for educational use—suitable for use by students at school, college and elsewhere. The directory also lists podcasts produced and published by pupils, young people, and educators.

MORE PODCAST DIRECTORIES

Here's a short list of a few directories you might want to visit. Each directory contains a little different list of podcast sites. All change quite frequently.

AllPodcasts: www.allpodcasts.com

BlogUniverse Podcast Directory: http://bloguniverse.com

Digital Podcast: www.digitalpodcast.com

Fresh Podcasts: www.freshpodcasts.com

Lusocast: www.lusocast.com (Portuguese directory)

Pod Lounge: www.thepodlounge.com

PodBlaze: www.podblaze.com

Podcast Bunker: www.podcastbunker.com

Podcast Directory: www.podcastdirectory.com

Podcast Empire: www.podcastempire.com

Podcast Videos: www.podcastvideos.org

Podcast.net: www.podcast.net

Podcasting Station: www.podcasting-station.com

PodSonoro: www.podsonoro.com (Spanish podcast search engine)

Syndic8 Podcasts: www.syndic8.com/podcasts/

Triyo: www.triyo.com

VodStock: www.vodstock.com

National Educational Technology Standards

National Educational Technology Standards for Students (NETS•S)

The National Educational Technology Standards for students are divided into six broad categories. Standards within each category are to be introduced, reinforced, and mastered by students. Teachers can use these standards as guidelines for planning technology-based activities in which students achieve success in learning, communication, and life skills.

1. **Basic operations and concepts**

   › Students demonstrate a sound understanding of the nature and operation of technology systems.

   › Students are proficient in the use of technology.

2. **Social, ethical, and human issues**

   › Students understand the ethical, cultural, and societal issues related to technology.

   › Students practice responsible use of technology systems, information, and software.

   › Students develop positive attitudes toward technology uses that support lifelong learning, collaboration, personal pursuits, and productivity.

3. **Technology productivity tools**

   › Students use technology tools to enhance learning, increase productivity, and promote creativity.

> Students use productivity tools to collaborate in constructing technology-enhanced models, preparing publications, and producing other creative works.

4. **Technology communications tools**

> Students use telecommunications to collaborate, publish, and interact with peers, experts, and other audiences.

> Students use a variety of media and formats to communicate information and ideas effectively to multiple audiences.

5. **Technology research tools**

> Students use technology to locate, evaluate, and collect information from a variety of sources.

> Students use technology tools to process data and report results.

> Students evaluate and select new information resources and technological innovations based on the appropriateness to specific tasks.

6. **Technology problem-solving and decision-making tools**

> Students use technology resources for solving problems and making informed decisions.

> Students employ technology in the development of strategies for solving problems in the real world.

National Educational Technology Standards for Teachers (NETS•T)

All classroom teachers should be prepared to meet the following standards and performance indicators.

I. Technology Operations and Concepts

Teachers demonstrate a sound understanding of technology operations and concepts. Teachers:

A. demonstrate introductory knowledge, skills, and understanding of concepts related to technology (as described in the ISTE National Educational Technology Standards for Students).

B. demonstrate continual growth in technology knowledge and skills to stay abreast of current and emerging technologies.

II. Planning and Designing Learning Environments and Experiences

Teachers plan and design effective learning environments and experiences supported by technology. Teachers:

A. design developmentally appropriate learning opportunities that apply technology-enhanced instructional strategies to support the diverse needs of learners.

B. apply current research on teaching and learning with technology when planning learning environments and experiences.

C. identify and locate technology resources and evaluate them for accuracy and suitability.

D. plan for the management of technology resources within the context of learning activities.

    E. plan strategies to manage student learning in a technology-enhanced environment.

III. Teaching, Learning, and the Curriculum

Teachers implement curriculum plans that include methods and strategies for applying technology to maximize student learning. Teachers:

    A. facilitate technology-enhanced experiences that address content standards and student technology standards.

    B. use technology to support learner-centered strategies that address the diverse needs of students.

    C. apply technology to develop students' higher-order skills and creativity.

    D. manage student learning activities in a technology-enhanced environment.

IV. Assessment and Evaluation

Teachers apply technology to facilitate a variety of effective assessment and evaluation strategies. Teachers:

    A. apply technology in assessing student learning of subject matter using a variety of assessment techniques.

    B. use technology resources to collect and analyze data, interpret results, and communicate findings to improve instructional practice and maximize student learning.

    C. apply multiple methods of evaluation to determine students' appropriate use of technology resources for learning, communication, and productivity.

V. Productivity and Professional Practice

Teachers use technology to enhance their productivity and professional practice. Teachers:

    A. use technology resources to engage in ongoing professional development and lifelong learning.

B. continually evaluate and reflect on professional practice to make informed decisions regarding the use of technology in support of student learning.

C. apply technology to increase productivity.

D. use technology to communicate and collaborate with peers, parents, and the larger community in order to nurture student learning.

VI. Social, Ethical, Legal, and Human Issues

Teachers understand the social, ethical, legal, and human issues surrounding the use of technology in PK–12 schools and apply that understanding in practice. Teachers:

A. model and teach legal and ethical practice related to technology use.

B. apply technology resources to enable and empower learners with diverse backgrounds, characteristics, and abilities.

C. identify and use technology resources that affirm diversity.

D. promote safe and healthy use of technology resources.

E. facilitate equitable access to technology resources for all students.